301
GREAT 1
MANAGEMENT IDEAS
from America's
Most Innovative Small Companies

Inc.
MAGAZINE

301
GREAT
MANAGEMENT IDEAS

from America's
Most Innovative Small Companies

INTRODUCTION BY TOM PETERS

edited by

SARA P. NOBLE

FOREWORD BY JEFFREY L. SEGLIN

301 Great Management Ideas
from America's
Most Innovative Small Companies

Designers: Brady and Paul Communications
& Robert Lesser

Portions of this book were originally
published in Inc. magazine.

This publication is designed to
provide accurate and authoritative
information in regard to the subject
matter covered. It is sold with
the understanding that the publisher
is not engaged in rendering
legal, accounting, or other professional
service. If legal advice or other expert
assistance is required, the services of a
competent professional
person should be sought.

Library of Congress
Catalog Card #: 91-72606

ISBN 0-9626146-4-5 (Paper)
ISBN 0-9626146-5-3 (Hardcover)

ACKNOWLEDGEMENTS

Some of us in our work lives are lucky enough to have worked with truly special people who we genuinely respect and enjoy. For me, working with the people at *Inc.* magazine was just such an experience. All of these people, past and present, deserve applause for producing a great magazine over the past 12 years.

There are some who deserve special recognition here for reporting, writing and editing the items which appear in this book. Unfortunately, space does not allow for naming everyone over the years, but those currently at the magazine include: Sara Baer-Sinnott, Alessandra Bianchi, Leslie Brokaw, Bo Burlingham, John Case, Elizabeth Conlin, Jay Finegan, Jill Andresky Fraser, Susan Greco, Michael Hopkins, Joshua Hyatt, Teri Lammers, Nancy Lyons, Robert Mamis, Martha Mangelsdorf, Anne Murphy, Bruce Posner, Tom Richman and Ellyn Spragins. Without their hard work and talents, the "Hands On" section of the magazine, where these items were originally published, would not have become so popular and indispensable to its readers month after month.

Also at *Inc.*, the support and enthusiasm of Robert LaPointe, Jan Spiro and Mary Ellen Mullaney of *Inc.* Subsidiary Publishing were greatly appreciated.

Outside of *Inc.*, thanks go to Robert Lesser of Brady and Paul Communications for his fine book design and tireless efforts, and Edward Coleman for his impeccable inputting.

Most importantly, credit goes to two editors. First, Jeffrey Seglin, the current editor of the "Hands On" section, who as a friend and talented work colleague, helped conceive and guide this book through to completion. And lastly, George Gendron, Editor-In-Chief of *Inc.*, a great editor and more. Without his creativity and endless supply of original ideas, *Inc.* magazine and this book would be far less inspired.

Sara P. Noble, Editor
Scituate, Mass., April 1991

Contents

Thanks to a crazy lifestyle, and an overlooked schedule conflict, I recently had to take a private charter aircraft from Toronto to Glens Falls, New York. More or less.

Fifteen minutes out of Toronto, smoke began to fill the cabin. The cautious pilot (the best kind) made an emergency landing in Buffalo — it seemed as though half the city's fire brigade, not to mention TV "anchors", met us.

Aircraft are phenomenally complex. Frankly, I'm surprised that such problems don't occur more frequently. In any event, though I don't know where any blame should be assigned, I'm not upset by the incident; it's the price of doing business on the run.

But let me tell you, I'm still fuming a year later about a full-fare, first-class American Airlines flight from Chicago to San Francisco — where "catering" didn't even include a second bag of peanuts!

BY TOM PETERS

Nuts, I say! (And said on TV.)

A brush with death (to overstate only a bit) — I can handle that. But "no peanuts" is intolerable; the memory does — and will — linger on.

"God is in the details." "Retail is detail." There are a hundred like statements. We nod. "Yup." But then, when we come across a Walt Disney, a Sewell Village Cadillac, a Stew Leonard (yes, the "usual suspects" — but that doesn't mean they don't deserve the acclaim), well, then, we know exactly what "passion for detail" is all about.

I've developed a theory over the years, and you'd be hard-pressed to dislodge it: In short, the essence of <u>sustainable</u> competitive advantage is 1) the obvious, (2) the little things, and (3) the accumulation of little things over the years.

It turns out that "hard to copy" is easy to copy. And "easy to copy" is hard to copy. Think about it.

A thriving <u>self</u>-serve gas station owner in Northern California is going gangbusters. One of his tricks: <u>He</u> pumps the gas. Hey, you can <u>see</u> it. Why can't the bamboozled competitor across the road "copy" him? (It's been going on for years.) "Beats me," says the puzzled (and successful) station owner.

The "stuff" that comes out of labs — even at a Merck — will be emulated in a couple of years (or less) by a passel of competitors. But a swift <u>process</u> of product development, say, consisting of an attitude of speed and a thousand telling details — that's a very different story.

In short, <u>competitive advantage that sticks</u> is invariably about a hundred, a thousand, a thousand-thousand tiny details — each readily copyable (<u>if</u> taken seriously by competitors, which is unusual and my point), but cumulatively extraordinary in impact, and virtually <u>un</u>copyable in practice. That is, all of the little things consistently done well create a company that defies duplication.

But is this relevant to smaller businesses?

You bet! A smaller business, to be sure, usually one-ups rivals with initial cleverness — a newfangled software spreadsheet, a novel restaurant format. To do so is no small feat. (Most don't get that far.) But today, at least, such cleverness will buy you a year or two of grace at most. The trick — yes, the trick — to sustainability lies, almost entirely, in being obsessed with constant improvement, eventually institutionalizing constant improvement.

Incidentally, I know all too well of what I speak. I run a small business. Our edge, we boast (only to ourselves), is "leading-edge ideas." It may or may not be true, but one thing is sure: A lot of competitors beat us through an absorbing attention to details. "Dullards," "laggards," we secretly call them — in the same way that Control Data and Sperry called IBM a dull laggard in the 1960s.

Hmmmmm!? Maybe I'd better read this book.

Who says good ideas have to cost big bucks? In the pages that follow, you'll find 301 great management ideas — the best ideas from America's most innovative companies, companies we write about regularly in the pages of *Inc.* magazine. Since its founding in 1979, owners of small to midsize companies have turned to *Inc.* for inspiring and innovative ideas on how to run their companies. With stories on startups, successes, and failures, *Inc.* has become an invaluable source on growing a business.

A quick word on the format of this book. The management tips are presented in bite-size pieces, one idea per page, 301 in all and divided by discipline into 36 chapters. We don't expect you to read cover to cover in one sitting, but to jump around, come back to ideas you've flagged, skip ahead to a section that has particular relevance to a problem you're trying to solve in your company.

BY JEFFREY L. SEGLIN

Senior Editor, Inc. magazine

These ideas come from a monthly department in *Inc.* called "Hands On, A Manager's Notebook." "Hands On" is about managing all aspects of business with little or no resources. You'll be stunned, surprised, and delighted to find ideas you can put into place in your own business tomorrow with relatively little capital or effort.

Readers turn to "Hands On" first, rip it out, pass it around to managers. They also copy the ideas with liberty. We run into countless businesses that have adapted an idea from "Hands On" and successfully implemented it themselves. These ideas work.

There are some items that simply grab the attention of *Inc.*'s 2.2 million readers more than others. These we've highlighted, one per chapter, with a stamp we call "Reader's Choice," indicating that these are the items which drew the biggest response from readers and that we see most copied out in the world of business. My personal favorite? The company in Erie, Pa., that invests $2 to have each prospective customer's photo taken when he visits the company and then packages the photo with a cover letter reminding the prospect why he came. The investment? Minor. The payoff? Increased customer responsiveness, not to mention some sales.

These are the best "Hands On" ideas we've ever come across — ideas based on real company efforts that have worked, most often with dramatic results. The items are reprinted here as they appeared in the magazine with some minor editing. We have not updated company revenues, locations, or employee numbers, because we figure a good idea is a good idea. In fact, we dare you to come up with better ones.

We're serious. To put our magazine where our mouth is, we're inviting you to enter our Idea Sweepstakes. The back page of 301 Great Management Ideas is your entry form. You think you have better management ideas that you use in your own company? Send them in. Copy the form, add extra sheets if you need them, share it with other employees of your company, compete with other divisions, turn it into a companywide contest to boost morale if you like, but get your ideas in to us.

You'll compete with companies across the country. The company that submits the best ideas, as judged by a panel of *Inc.* Editors, will have the ideas as well as a picture of their entire company published in *Inc.* In addition, Tom Peters will extend a free admission for one at his management "Skunk Camp".

So read on. Absorb. Delight in the practical wisdom of hundreds of smart businesses. Put these proven ideas into practice in your own company and watch the results. And tell us how you're doing. We're always on the look out for a few smart companies.

"The founder of a business
gets to a point where his or her
personal growth is
much more involved with allowing
others in the company to grow,
so that they can give meaning
to their own lives."

PAUL HAWKEN,
CEO, Smith & Hawken

Their Brothers' Keepers

There's no more common management pitfall than to spend most of your time with the weaker people in your organization, leaving the strong to fend for themselves. Invariably, the company suffers. While the lackluster performers may improve marginally, the people who could really deliver for you are deprived of the leadership they need. Problem is, it's often hard to avoid **dealing with stragglers**, who - by definition - need help. After all, if you don't do it, who will?

Well, maybe their more capable peers, says Gary Blumenthal, president of Tinderbox International Inc., a franchisor of tobacco and gift stores, based in Los Angeles. He has formed a group called "The Committee of 90," representing the company's solid performers. The members meet four times a year, discussing various issues and sharing techniques they have tried in their stores. Then Blumenthal assigns them to visit other outlets, where they advise franchisees with problems.

"It builds a feeling of co-responsibility," he says. "From their peers, the advice is both much less threatening and much more embarrassing."

1

House Rules

Most company presidents pay lip service to employee participation, but few go as far as Frederick Shaltz Jr., president of Delta Land Surveying & Engineering Inc., in Flint, Mich. At least once a year, he asks his 23 employees to vote on such issues as bonuses, tardiness penalties, choice of insurance, and dress codes. Last August, moonlighting was ruled out by a vote of 18 to 5. Around the December holidays, the employees were expected to ban smoking - even though Shaltz is a smoker. After each vote, the decision or rule is entered in the **employee handbook**, known as the *Blue Book*.

The *Blue Book*, says Shaltz, provides a framework for constructive decision making, fosters teamwork, and eliminates divisive complaining. As soon as an issue presents itself, a vote is taken. Shaltz credits the book with keeping the firm efficient: "Thanks to the *Blue Book*, these 23 people are doing the work that would normally take 27 or 30 people. I'm intent on having them involved in the business as much as possible."

2

A Glimpse to the Other Side

The birth of Bread Loaf Construction Co.'s **Employee of the Month program** was certainly inauspicious. Leo Breshnahan, a field worker, had approached executive vice-president John Leehman at the company's annual meeting for its 160 employees and complained: "We do all the work out in the field, while people in the office are just having a good time."

Leehman invited Breshnahan to spend the day seeing how the office crew earns a living. "It was a real turning point for Breshnahan," says Leehman. "He knows where he can go in the system, and so do other employees who have followed in his footsteps."

Now, every month an employee is chosen to tour Bread Loaf's offices and construction sites to get a sense of just what other people do in the corporation.

What's more, spending a day with the star employee gives managers of the Middlebury, Vt., business a chance to get acquainted with the best management candidates in the company.

3

The Buddy System

The biggest complaint about hourly employees - especially if they're teenagers or college students - is that they often don't show up for work. Well, Lisa G. Renshaw, who runs four parking lots in Baltimore, hires college students almost exclusively, and she never has that problem. Her secret: the buddy system.

"For every shift, I'll **assign two people for each job**," says Renshaw, president of 13-employee Penn Parking. "You'll have the 2:30 p.m. to 10:30 p.m. shift Monday through Wednesday, and I'll have it Thursday through Sunday, and you and I will be buddies. If I can't cover my shift, I can call you up and switch. And you can do the same for me."

Rarely can both people not make it, says Renshaw. "People are more than willing to cover for their buddies because they know that someday they'll want them to return the favor."

4

Write It Down (Right Away)

To be sure his company won't lose the ideas its employees come up with, William Donahoo, CEO of Clinch River Corp., provides every worker with a special **pocket notebook for recording suggestions**.

Donahoo was overwhelmed by suggestions when his company bought a Harriman, Tenn., paperboard plant and rehired laid-off workers. So he passed out three-by-five-inch notebooks marked, "Good Ideas for Clinch River."

Each week management lists each suggestion, the employee who made it, and its status. "In eight weeks, we got more than 100 ideas," Donahoo says. Nearly half of them are already being implemented.

5

Employees Just Want to Have Fun

An extensive, company-sponsored recreation and social program can be a boon to morale - but it can also be a fiscal and managerial nightmare to the CEO who has to administer it. Jack Stack, CEO of Springfield Remanufacturing Center Corp., in Springfield, Mo., was so intent on fostering healthy relations with his 450 employees that he began feeling more like a camp director with each passing athletic season. His solution? Set a budget, and then let your employees divvy it up themselves.

"It's really hard to please everybody," says Stack. "You don't know how to draw the line and be fair at the same time." So he established a **recreation committee** for each of his plants. Eight employees, elected annually, receive a budget of $5,000 with which to fund company softball and volleyball teams, fishing tournaments, and a company picnic. "It gets rid of the little headaches for managers," Stack says, "and it gives employees a taste of what it's like to be a manager."

6

People's Court

An informal employee-grievance policy isn't good enough for American Steel & Wire Corp., in Cuyahoga Heights, Ohio. At this 540-employee business, compensation, promotion, and termination beefs are taken to an **employee council that reviews managers' decisions**. "We wanted a formal way to resolve issues with employees that would be objective and give them confidence in the management team here," says CEO Tom Tyrrell.

Termination disputes can go directly to the council, but employees must work through a chain of management command for all other grievances. From a pool of employee volunteers trained in arbitration, the complainant blindly chooses nine names and then picks the six employees and one manager who will hear his case. In the past year and a half the council has heard 30 cases. About 50% of the judgments have upheld the manager's original decision.

7

Attendance Required

Employee absenteeism costs companies millions of dollars every year in lost productivity and/or increased overtime costs, but ask a manager to quantify the problem - how many days are missed, who misses them, when the absences occur most frequently and it is likely you won't get any definite answers. The vast majority of companies don't keep tabs on employee attendance, and that in itself is part of the problem, says Joel Levy, of Coopers & Lybrand in New York City. "You can't solve your Friday problem, unless you know you have a Friday problem."

Education Computer Corp. knew it had a problem, and chose to address it by making attendance a formal part of its employee-appraisal system. The manufacturer of training simulators, headquartered in Strafford, Pa., tracks its employees by the week, then provides supervisors with detailed attendance reports every six months. Employees who don't regularly come to work risk losing pay hikes, or, if unexcused absences aren't eliminated, their jobs.

The Liebert Corp., a manufacturer of environmental control systems for data-processing installations in Columbus, Ohio, takes a different approach, using rewards as the motivation. The company gives hourly employees three shares of company stock for each year of perfect attendance and two free movie tickets for each unblemished quarter.

Ugly Duckling Rent-A-Car System, Inc., headquartered in Tucson, checks applicants' past attendance records as part of the reference-checking process. As president Thomas S. Duck Sr. says, "The best way to solve an absenteeism problem is not to have any absenteeism to begin with."

8

Sponsoring a New Hire

F irst impressions last, which is why it pays to think about **how new employees are introduced to your company**. The way new hires are handled during their initial weeks on the job will go far toward determining whether they'll become productive, enthusiastic contributors. With this in mind, Sequent Computer Systems, Inc. doesn't leave anything to chance.

Every new employee of the Beaverton, Ore., company is assigned to a sponsor even before his or her first day of work. The sponsor is charged with taking the new recruit through Sequent's main streets and back roads - introducing the employee to others, rounding up office supplies, training the new hire on the electronic mail system, and imparting various aspects of company culture.

Sponsors, who volunteer for the assignments, commit about 30 minutes a day to their adoptees over the first couple of weeks. Sequent is convinced that the cost of losing the daily half-hour of labor is far exceeded by the program's benefits. "One of the main values of this company is teamwork," says Barbara Gaffney, vice-president for human resources. "New employees work better if they know the other players, and a sponsor is one way they get to know people faster."

READER'S CHOICE

9

Getting to Know You

Your business is growing, your staff is getting bigger - and you know less and less about each employee. What's more, they probably don't know much about one another. One way to attack the problem and celebrate your people? **A company yearbook**.

That's what Original Copy Centers Inc., in Cleveland, decided its three-shift, 110-person staff could use. The execution is simple: everybody fills out questionnaires asking about their favorite music, ideal weekend, biggest challenges, and best childhood memory. Other fill-in-the blanks: "What I really like about my job" and "My role at Original." The book devotes a full page to each person's quotes, which run alongside a large photo.

While the yearbook is for employees, marketing manager Michael Setta says that customers also browse through the books, which are displayed in the lobby of the company's headquarters. And company president Nancy Vetrone, who conducts all the annual reviews, uses the profiles as back-ground.

Production, done in-house, costs about $1,600, mostly for photography. If Original had to pay for everything, Setta estimates, the tab would be closer to $5,000.

10

Suggestion Sweepstakes

S how us a company with an employee suggestion box, and we'll show you a company that is desperately in need of suggestions, the first one being: **get rid of that suggestion box**. We've almost never seen one that worked. Managers seldom have time to read the suggestions, and an ignored suggestion is worse than none at all.

The paradox is that employees often *do* have the best ideas for improving a company. Consider Springfield Remanufacturing Center Inc., where a single employee has come up with production suggestions that have saved the company about $2 million.

If you don't have the staff or the resources to keep up a credible, ongoing suggestion program, you might want to take a tip from Betsy Howe of Howe Communications, a suggestion specialist in West Boylston, Mass. Her approach involves setting up a specific program of limited duration (say, six weeks) with rewards for the best ideas each week, and a grand prize at the program's end. Even if you don't wind up with million-dollar suggestions, you just might do something for morale.

11

Targeting Outplacements

Nobody likes to lose a good employee, but let's face it: sooner or later, **some of your best employees are going to outgrow your company**. The danger is that they may leave for one of your competitors. What's the alternative? "I try to get them better jobs with vendors," says Judson Beamsley, founder and president of Tek-Aids Industries Inc., a $24-million distributor of microcomputer products, based in Arlington Heights, Ill.

Beamsley says that he encourages employees to talk openly about their job aspirations. "If someone wants to leave, I'll give him a recommendation." He estimates that, in the past eight years, he's helped 25 employees find new jobs - which is a lot, considering that Tek-Aids employs only 42 people. By playing such an active role, Beamsley not only keeps good people away from his competitors, he also builds a network of company alumni who tell him about developments in the market. "If I didn't already know what my competitors were doing, I could find out very quickly."

12

Let Your Client Be the Judge

At most companies, it's an annual rite for employees to sit down with their bosses and review their strengths and weaknesses. After all, who can better **judge employees' performance** than their immediate superiors?

Warren Rodgers can think of some. Why not let employees rate themselves? says the president of Computer Specialists Inc., in Monroeville, Pa. And if you're in a service business, you may be overlooking an obvious critic: your clients. They may see your employees more often - and in a greater variety of circumstances - than you do.

Twice a year, Rodgers asks his clients and each of his 150 employees to fill out evaluation forms. Then, he and the employee compare the two evaluations. "If people feel the quality of their work is an 8 out of 10, and the client feels it's a 4, there's trouble," says Rodgers.

13

Thanks for a Job Well Done

There's only one way to **show appreciation for the extraordinary efforts** of employees: do something extraordinary in return. Joseph and Laurie Cherry do just that for the employees of Cherry Tire Service Inc., in Maybrook, N.Y., a truck-tire road-service company. The benefit: an annual, all-expenses-paid weekend in the Poconos.

Every employee who has worked two or more years at Cherry Tire is entitled to take his or her spouse to Caesars Pocono Resorts in Lakeville, Pa., where the company provides the couple with a suite for the weekend. Each year, the company upgrades the suite - right up to the Champagne Towers with a Jacuzzi shaped like a seven-foot champagne glass and a heart-shaped swimming pool in the room. "The upgrading gives everybody something new to look forward to," says Joe Cherry. "When they come back, they are different people."

The benefit reflects Cherry's approach to management. "These guys work very hard at dangerous jobs. The reason they work hard is that they want a better life. We owe them a salary, just like they owe us the work, but the weekend is different. We're saying, 'This weekend is for you. Take it.' It's worth more psychologically than the $600 or $700 it costs."

14

Family Ties

In busy times, it's standard practice to ask employees to work overtime and pay them for it. But Rick Johnson, founder and CEO of BurJon Steel Service Center Inc., in Springboro, Ohio, feels that when the company requires a great deal of overtime for long stretches, money alone isn't enough. On the theory that families and friends suffer when people spend that much time at work, he augments overtime pay with flowers and coupons for dinner at a local restaurant.

Usually Johnson sends the **flowers and dinner coupons directly to the employee's spouse** or to a friend, along with a personal note. "When somebody works hard, it's hard on everyone," he says. "We think it's important to say thanks."

15

A Message From Above

In any growing business, the day comes when the **founder no longer knows everybody in the company**. That's a loss for him, and a danger for the company, since it usually signifies a weakening of the bonds that have helped the business grow in the first place.

At Koss Corp., in Milwaukee, chairman John Koss mitigates the problem by going to see each employee on his or her birthday and delivering a greeting card containing a gift certificate to the company store. The gift certificate is worth $5 for each year of tenure, amounting to as much as $100 for a longtime employee. In addition, employees get a 50% discount at the company store. Aside from ensuring direct contact between Koss and his 175 employees, the program makes it possible for hourly workers to buy Koss's products, which they otherwise might not be able to afford. (Koss's top-of-the-line stereo headphones sell for up to $175.)

"The response has been tremendous," says personnel director Michael Moore, who dreamed up the program. Not only has morale improved, but the company store - previously little used by employees - now does a booming business.

16

Employee of the Month

Keeping participative-management promises with employees can be tricky. How can a manager delegate work and then give employees recognition for a job well done without making it sound as if it's coming down from on high? At Meridian Travel Inc., in Cleveland, CEO Cynthia Bender opted for a participative solution: **turn pat-on-the-back duties over to the employees**.

Once a month all 62 employees of the $21-million company write in their vote for who should be Employee of the Month. "Managers always have their favorites, but the employees know who pitches in and helps out," says Bender.

"It's important different departments don't become isolated," she says. "This makes employees notice others more and develops camaraderie."

COMMUNICATIONS

"If you want to know what's really
going on in most companies,
you talk to the guy who sweeps the floors.
Nine times out of 10, he knows more
than the president. So I make a point
of knowing what my floor
sweepers know – even if it means
sweeping the floors."

KENNETH A. HENDRICKS,
CEO, ABC Supply Co., #1 INC. 500 Co. in 1986

Solving Interdepartmental Short Circuits

As SynOptics Communications, a supplier of computer-networking systems, grew from 11 to 425 employees over four years, communications problems among the company's five functional groups grew just as fast. So CEO Andrew Ludwick began the "**staff-to-staff brown bag lunch**."

The idea for the lunch meetings came after a manufacturing line supervisor complained that a new circuit board took much too long to assemble. Ludwick sat the supervisor and an engineer down at the same table to figure out how they could work together to make the product easier to assemble. By replacing a part on the board with a smaller, cheaper part, they determined, the board could be assembled much more quickly.

Now, each quarter the company buys lunch for two related divisions. All the key people from both divisions sit down together at five tables in the company's Mountain View, Calif., headquarters. Each table is assigned a problem that it must solve over lunch and then present the results to the rest of the group.

"On a superficial level, we are simply solving problems," says Ludwick. "But we are also creating chemistry among all our employees."

18

Keeping in Touch With the Troops

The bigger your company grows, the harder it is to tell how employees feel about their jobs. "It's frustrating," says Lacy Edwards, president and chief executive of XA Systems Corp., a $13-million software maker in Los Gatos, Calif. "You just lose contact with people." To help his top executives and himself stay in touch with the rest of the company, Edwards inaugurated annual "skip-level" interviews.

Once a year, **employees have a one-on-one conversation with their boss's boss**. "How's your job going?" they are asked. "What can we do to make things better?"

"It gives you a legitimate opportunity to explore without going around somebody," says Edwards, who interviews everyone who reports to his six vice-presidents. He also discovered people who would be perfect for jobs elsewhere in the company. "It's a chance to get to know them a little," Edwards observes. "In a different environment, the interviews could be used to air dirty laundry. But the people here have confidence that they are doing a good job."

19

Addressing the Issues

I f your business has many branches or locations and is growing at a rapid pace, how can you possibly manage to communicate with all of your employees? Try publishing a **booklet that highlights the events of the meetings held at every company branch** and location and distributing it to all employees.

Once each quarter several executives of Staples Inc., a $120-million discount office-supply chain based in Newton, Mass., meet with employees at each of the company's 34 stores. They talk about the company's performance and the priorities for the months ahead, pick one problem area, and solicit suggestions.

Employees also get a chance to ask questions and raise any other issues of concern. A month later Staples distributes to all its employees a booklet featuring answers to the most commonly asked questions at each meeting, as well as additional company news and information.

"The meetings make people feel that management is interested in them and in the best ways to do things," says Todd Krasnow, vice-president of marketing. The booklet ensures that everyone at all of the company's branches gets to share in that employee wisdom.

20

Pet Peeve Management

How can you help employees feel more comfortable approaching one another when they're unhappy about something?

Every other month Pat Bruner, president of the two-site T.L.C. Child Care Centers Inc., takes her 22 employees out for pizza. The first hour is open season for criticism about anything and anybody, including management. Protests range from "You borrowed my supplies without returning them" to "You get too tense when things get crazy." The second hour is devoted to positive comments and finding solutions to issues raised. Out in Green Bay, Wis., the cost of these **formal gripe sessions** is a measly $35 to $50.

21

Seeing is Believing

"After a tough time growing this company, people felt like quitting," says Valarie Wilson, chairman and CEO of Wilson Sculley Associates Inc., a St. Louis advertising firm. "They wondered what all their hard work was for." Once a quarter, Wilson lifts sagging spirits with a Saturday morning QUIT (quarterly internal talks) meeting.

Six meetings and one and a half years later, not one of her employees has quit.

Wilson believes that by **seeing the numbers and plans typically reserved for board members**, employees know exactly where they fit in. But she's convinced that it's the entertaining and often-offbeat presentations that really make the Saturday morning meetings work. At one quarterly meeting that used a sports motif, managers announced lineup changes in the organization chart; posted scores for profitability, sales, and overhead for the first half of the year; and unveiled the strategy for the second half of the year.

Why hold meetings on Saturday? Employees aren't distracted then, notes Wilson, who has seen the company grow from $8.8 million in billings to $15 million in one year.

22

Mail Call

Want to keep close tabs on just how your company's doing? You're probably delegating away one **valuable source of information: the daily mail**.

Don't underestimate it, say the folks at Paramount Flag Co., a $1.2-million San Francisco flag manufacturer. Each morning the seven managers gather and open each piece. "There's a definite pleasure in seeing what's in the envelope," says Christophe Morin, Paramount's president. "If it's a purchase order, great. If it's a big bill from a supplier, we'll look at why it's so high. If someone's returning a $2 flag, everybody understands how important details are to the future of the company."

But isn't the managers' time really better spent on other matters? Nope, Morin says. "It only takes half an hour, 45 minutes at most. And we never have to have formal meetings, because we get together every day." The idea, by the way, came from Paramount's parent company, Doublet, a $30-million French manufacturer where executives still chip in every morning at mail time.

23

What's <u>Really</u> on Your Mind?

Want to keep up with what your employees really think? Establish an **employee sounding board**, says Sally Tassani, founder of Tassani Communications Inc., in Chicago.

Tassani came upon the idea haphazardly. "There I was in a meeting with my key managers trying to figure out what employees wanted," she says. "I realized I should ask them myself. Boy, was I surprised." She learned in her first meeting with employees that a benefits package she had been agonizing over wasn't worth the effort. What they really wanted was more access, inspiration, and positive reinforcement from their managers. These were at least as important as a better bonus system.

"The meeting was so successful that I decided to do it on a regular basis," Tassani says. Now, she meets with a board of about 10 employees twice monthly.

To create the board, each department head recommended a non-managerial employee who has good communication skills and was caught up on work. The board even includes the company's clerical workers. "It eats up about an hour every other week, so I want the most efficient, bright, and capable employees," Tassani says.

24

An Alternative to Meetings

Even in small companies it's a struggle to keep employees informed. Bob Cummins, president of Fargo Electronics, a $6-million Eden Prairie, Minn., specialty printer manufacturer, countered his 28 employees' threat of daily meetings with a charged idea: **a daily electronic newsletter**, which he was sure could be faster *and* more informative.

At day's end, department heads jot messages into the company's electronic-mail system. The next morning the file is printed out and copies of the "newsletter" are put in the break room. Regular topics include daily sales and production figures, profit-sharing updates, and customer feedback. "It's been great for eliminating surprises," says Cummins. "If problems with a product keep coming up in the newsletter, no one's shocked when we discontinue it."

25

Culture Clash

How do managers who are used to working with corporate employees in three-piece suits and wing tips deal with the company's more creative types - those software engineers, copywriters, scientists, and art directors who tend to show up at work on bicycles, in tennis shoes and blue jeans, with dogs?

Some managers may decide, in the interest of peace and harmony, to keep their creative divisions as separate from the business side as possible. Integrated Genetics Inc. took a different tack and living up to its name, **integrates its business and creative divisions**. The $5-million bio-engineering company in Framingham, Mass., devised a strategy "to prevent the scientists from becoming an esoteric group shut off from the company", says Pat Connoy, vice-president of sales and marketing. Each Friday, one of the scientists gives a presentation to the company at large, on subjects ranging from his own in-house work to a new development in biotechnology. Once a month an employee from the selling, marketing, or administrative side takes a turn speaking to the scientists on anything from finance to strategic planning. The company also runs a weekly in-house seminar called "Science for Non-Scientists," in which scientists explain their work in detail to the administrative employees. "The formation of corporate cliques, with their own little cultures, is a danger at companies like ours," says Connoy.

Fostering Teamwork

As companies grow, it isn't easy to stay up on what everyone's doing. Opportunities for teamwork often get lost. Norman Howe, CEO of Norman Howe & Associates, a marketing and consulting business in Pasadena, Calif., has developed a system to combat these kinds of inefficiencies. It's built around a **weekly "to do" list**.

Every Monday morning, Howe's 26 employees make lists of their tasks or projects. The lists are then shared with supervisors and read at a staff lunch.

A big advantage to operating this way, Howe says, is the team atmosphere it creates. "People have a more complete view of what's happening." Frequently, he notes, individuals suggest new ways to approach problems; if they have time, they even offer to help colleagues in a pinch. The staff lunches usually last about an hour, Howe says. "There's a real value in articulating what you're working on to a group."

READER'S CHOICE

27

Know Thine Enemy

How much should your employees know about your competition? A lot, according to Federal Express. The company's monthly internal newsletter includes two columns devoted to telling all: "Newsview," which excerpts dozens of published clips about Federal Express and its competitors, and "Competitive Corner," which has updates on the competition and tells "what Federal Express is doing to keep ahead of the enemy."

Employees learn about such happenings as United Parcel Service's test of a radio dispatch system and a gossip column's report that Jack Nicholson uses Fed Ex to get videotapes of Los Angeles Lakers games. Newsletter editor Carolyn Gause says employee surveys show that stories about competitors are among the best-read items in the publication. And at the same time that they provide some fun, she adds, the columns help employees become better informed about the industry.

Food for Thought

I f you want your people to focus on performance, you've got to figure out an effective way to tell them how the company is doing. Jay Johnson lets his people's palates do the talking. Every month, he holds a communication session for the 70 employees of Crest Microfilm Inc., in Cedar Rapids, Iowa. If it's been a so-so month, he orders pizza and soft drinks. But if the company has done well, he lets the employees choose the cuisine. "In a bad month, we'll spend $75 or $80," says Johnson, "and in a good month, $250. At year end, we may spend $450 if we've had as good a year as we'd hoped for."

Food aside, Johnson uses the occasion to talk about company performance. "I give a summary of why we're eating what we're eating, and employees have an opportunity to bring up complaints and suggestions. . . . It's a way for me to share what I'm thinking. It's also an opportunity for me to say, 'Thanks.' When everyone works hard, they *should* eat prime rib rather than pizza."

29

Explaining Financials

Sharing an income statement and balance sheet with the ranks can be a powerful tool for motivating performance, but not if employees don't understand them. So the financial statements at employee-owned Reflexite Corp., in New Britain, Conn., come complete with explanations for each line item.

The idea came from a discussion president and CEO Cecil Ursprung had with key managers. "One of my bright, capable managers said, 'I hope you publish something different from what I got, because I don't know how to read the thing,'" Ursprung says. "I thought, we'd better do some educating when we hand this out."

The annotations, for such items as prepaid expenses ("This is the value of expenses paid in advance, such as insurance premiums"), appear in fine print in the right-hand margin, close to the appropriate number and with a line connecting the two.

30

Outlet for Frustrations

CEOs like to believe they are open to employees' comments and ideas. Whether that's true is often hard to judge, but Rick Johnson, general manager of Vincent Metals, in Springboro, Ohio, doesn't want to leave it to chance. He put a locked box in the lunchroom in which frustrated employees can leave him messages - he has the only key.

The idea isn't to replace interaction between employees and supervisors. Rather, Johnson explains, "it's a safety valve for people who feel threatened or ignored." During the first six months it was in place, Johnson says, he got just a few messages. But the frequency of use doesn't begin to capture the value, he claims. "It's to show people they have a voice around here, that **everyone has a direct link to the top**."

31

"I'd rather have an employee
with half the academic credentials
and twice the team spirit,
because without that,
you've got nothing."

STAN BENTLEY,
Diversified Systems Inc.

Cloning Good Employees

Looking to cut both your recruiting costs and employee turnover? Maybe you should tap the folks who already make your company work - your employees.

At Integrated Microcomputer Systems Inc., a $20-million software development company in Rockville, Md., about 60% of its 400 workers have been hired through an **employee referral program**. The company's turnover rate is only 3%.

All jobs are posted at the company's seven client sites, and employees make referrals by filling out a standard form and attaching the applicant's resume. If the applicant is hired and remains on board at least four months, the referring worker gets a bonus - from $300 (for administrative jobs) to $800 (for technical positions). The bonus for filling senior or skilled positions has been as generous as $1,000 and a personal computer.

Personnel specialist Tammy Besser says the program has made for a better work atmosphere. "People recommend people they want to work with, people they trust. Good employees tend to recommend people with similar characteristics." Relatives are especially welcome, as company president John Yeh's example attests. To date, he's hired three of his brothers, one sister, and two sisters-in-law.

32

Discretion Required

Hiring top managers can be tricky, especially if the top candidates are employed by customers. "We've had recruitment firms offer their services, but they're too aggressive," says the president of a fast-growing technology consulting company. "We weren't certain they'd be discreet, and their fees were ridiculous."

Instead, he **assigned one of his own employees to be a part-time undercover headhunter**. Company executives make note of talented people they meet and actively maintain the contacts. When a position opens, they pass the name to the in-house headhunter, who makes the inquiry, using an obscure company name and a different phone number.

"Where we're unsure of our client's reaction, this is the best approach," says the president. "If we strike out, nobody knows we called." Should the potential recruit be interested, the headhunter reveals his true employer. Then negotiations begin in earnest.

Falsified Claims

Think you've finally found the perfect candidate to fill a position at your company? Be sure to check - and double-check - the information on the resume in front of you. There's a 30% chance that something will be wrong.

According to Barrick Security Group, a San Mateo, Calif., firm that does corporate investigative work, some of those job applicants exaggerate their work histories, and others make exaggerated education claims. About 3% omit criminal violations.

How can you improve your odds of getting the truth? Barrick president Barry Bergman advises managers to **have applicants fill out a standard job form** - which should include questions about criminal convictions - and to make it clear that responses will be checked. You don't need those riders in order to do a legal follow-up, he says, but "putting people on notice makes it less likely that a degree in political science will become an engineering degree, or that three months at a previous job will become three years."

34

Prospecting the Customer List

Shopsmith Inc., a $43-million Dayton manufacturer of woodworking equipment, may just have found the solution to the age-old problem of finding good employees who are knowledgeable about its products.

If a position opens up at one of its retail outlets or when it needs to hire staff for a new-store launch - the company has opened one store a month over the past three years - Shopsmith **sends letters and postcards to local customers** announcing it is looking for managers and part-time help.

The average direct-mail campaign to 3,000 customers costs at least 30% less than a classified ad in a local newspaper. It's been so successful that Shopsmith has stopped using classified ads altogether in some markets.

"It's the rifle versus the shotgun approach," as advertising director Perry Martin puts it. He reports that Shopsmith has found virtually all its part-time woodworkers and a handful of managers through the two-year-old campaign. For Shopsmith's loyal customers who sign on, says Martin, "it's their dream job."

READER'S CHOICE

35

Tapping the Big Boys

You say you're trying to grow your company? Where do you turn to find top-notch employees? Try the **human resources departments of corporations that are downsizing.** They'll send you free books filled with employees' resumes, from difficult-to-find factory floor workers to R&D engineers.

When Eric Giler, president of Brooktrout Technology Inc., a maker of electronic-messaging systems in Needham, Mass., doubled the payroll from 20 to 40 people in six months, he found five engineers that way. By not using a corporate headhunter, he estimates he saved $30,000. "It's tough to get hired by these companies," says Giler. "They've done a first cut for us."

36

Finding Their Own Replacements

Having **employees hire the people with whom they'll be working** can be the best way to ensure that teams function well together.

At Johnsonville Foods Inc., a manufacturer based in Sheboygan, Wis., employees who are promoted from merchandisers to salespeople hire their replacements. Because merchandisers work closely backing up the sales force and because so much of salespeople's compensation comes from performance bonuses, their hiring decisions dramatically affect how much money they make.

"I want people to learn how to get good people, how to coach them, what it takes to get good performance," CEO Ralph Stayer says. "They'll also learn lessons in bad hiring early on at a level where mistakes are chicken feed to the company."

Frame of Reference

Checking a job candidate's references has become a perfunctory task for many managers. Remarks are so general they become virtually meaningless. To find out what the terms *hard worker*, *detail-oriented*, and *people person* really mean to someone, managers at Octel Communications Corp., in Milpitas, Calif., spend up to an hour on the phone with at least three references per candidate, discussing not just the candidate, but also the **reference's own work ethic and corporate culture**.

"What we're trying to gauge is the frame of reference a person is using to provide an opinion" says president and CEO Robert Cohn. "It can be very revealing."

Cohn decided not to offer a job to one management candidate after a conversation with a key reference - a senior executive who exhibited poor people skills. Why? Cohn figures if the caliber of the references doesn't match Octel's expectations, there's a pretty good chance that the job candidate's won't either.

Apparently the method is working. Octel's employee attrition rate is 5%, twice as good as Silicon Valley standards, Cohn claims.

38

Finding a Good Listener

In an age of professional resumes, it's difficult to tell much about candidates you are interviewing. One way to assess them is to **have them write up "minutes" after a job interview**. Victoria Buyniski, CEO of $5-million United Medical Resources Inc., in Cincinnati, has used the approach to hire each of the 91 employees who staff her health-care-administration business - from the mail room to the executive suite.

Candidates who don't come off well in a face-to-face interview will often show promotable attributes in their writing, while others describe a job markedly different from what Buyniski has to offer, indicating potential communication problems.

"Three pages dashed off in 15 minutes tells me they are producers," she says. "Lots of cross-outs tell me that people couldn't even match their socks very easily."

Sniffing Out the Truth

The litigation explosion has made it harder to **check references on job applicants**, as previous employers grow nervous about possible lawsuits from their ex-employees. But there are things you can do to improve your chances of getting accurate information, according to Peter LeVine of Framingham, Mass., who has built a business as a professional reference-checker:

*Decide what you want to know in advance, and then ask all of your prepared questions before posing follow-up ones. That way, you'll be sure to get to the major points.

*Keep your questions neutral, so as not to offend, or lead, the reference. Don't ask, "Does he knuckle under pressure?" but rather, "How does he handle pressure?"

*Avoid mentioning the job until you've discussed the applicant. Otherwise, the reference will focus on the position, not the person.

*Don't waste time with personal references. "They've never seen the applicant in a work setting," says LeVine. In checking work references, moreover, don't just talk to the applicant's previous boss. Often the best information comes from peers, subordinates, and outsiders, such as suppliers, customers, or auditors.

*Check academic and previous job credentials. "If he's lied about those, I'll guarantee he's lied about things you can't verify."

40

Watch Your Language

Finding the right employee used to be the most difficult aspect of the hiring process. Making the offer itself was simple: You just dropped a letter in the mail.

Now, however, that **friendly letter welcoming the employee on board may be considered a binding contract**. Courts across the country have held, for example, that if a salary is stated as an annual amount the employee cannot be fired for a year. Or, if the letter says that the employee's performance will be reviewed in six months, then it is a contract to keep him or her on that long.

Joseph E. O'Leary, a lawyer at Choate, Hall & Stewart in Boston, advises his clients to include the employee's starting date, job title, salary, and benefits in an offer letter. But he suggests that salary should always be given in monthly terms. As to the timing of evaluations or raises, the letter should say, "Your performance and salary will be reviewed periodically." Also, benefits should not be downgraded, even if company policy changes, unless the letter states that perks are subject to modification.

Some employers, in their concern, have gone so far as to include such statements as "This letter does not constitute a specific term of employment," or, "This letter constitutes the entire agreement between us, and overrides any statements made during the interview process." But most lawyers advise against including harsh legalese, which can be off-putting to the potential employee.

41

Getting the Best Response

If you've searched for **ways to write a help-wanted classified** that will bring in the kind of responsible, conscientious candidates you'd like to interview, you might want to take your cue from Steve Kantor.

Kantor, president of Gnossos Software, in Washington, D.C., wrote an ad that brought five times more responses than the newspaper had told him to expect - about 175 in all - and turned up five finalists he would have been more than happy to hire.

The ad began, "Small entrepreneurial firm seeks sharp liberal arts grad. Vision, ethics, personality required." Kantor claims many of the candidates cited "ethics" as the reason they answered the ad.

Kantor then sent a congratulations-on-being-selected-for-consideration letter to the top 20% of the applicants and asked them to answer these questions in another letter: "What are your greatest strengths and weaknesses? What did you like and hate most about your most recent work experience? Describe the political, social, and economic impact of PCs." (Kantor says he was "half kidding" with the last question, and he was looking for respondents who answered in kind.)

"This way, I can screen out people who don't have drive and ambition," says Kantor, who ended up interviewing about 20 final candidates by phone. "I can get a feel for people without being influenced by their physical appearance, and it gives applicants a chance to be thoughtful about their responses. Plus, I save loads of time and energy."

42

Flexible Staffing

While 60% of all "temps" are still clerical workers, the use of professional temps is one of the fastest-growing areas in the temporary industry. These new temps include accountants, engineers, systems analysts - even nuclear plant designers.

By **hiring temporary professionals**, companies can save on costly benefits and can cut back their work force with much less trauma if business starts to slide. Temps also make sense when a company is facing reorganization, changes in office automation, or a new-product introduction.

Summa Four Inc., a manufacturer of telecommunications equipment in Manchester, N.H., has been using temporary designers and engineers for years. "There are time windows through which we must enter a product, or we lose a significant amount of sales," says David Prince, director of engineering. "That's why we use temps."

When U. S. Travel World, a Somerville, Mass., travel agency wanted to enter a new market, it hired a temporary marketing pro. "[The temp] helped us with a marketing strategy and an ad campaign," says partner Nicholas Salerno. "It really boils down to one-on-one service that - on our budget - we just wouldn't get from a regular ad agency."

Some companies even use temporary services as a source of people they may want to hire permanently. But as temporary-services agencies become more sophisticated - some offer technical training benefits and profit sharing - fewer temps are willing to abandon the flexibility for full-time jobs.

43

The Man on the Street

When you need unskilled or entry-level employees, one way to find them is embarrassingly simple: **pay attention to the general public you deal with every day**. Blair Brown, CEO of Charrette Corp., a chain of architecture- and design-supply stores based in metropolitan Boston, considers everyone he meets in passing as a possible Charrette staff member. "I told my personnel department they have to develop guerrilla strategies so the business can grow," Brown says. To date, the tactic has paid off in the hiring of eight people - good results, considering its beginnings.

When Brown's car broke down during a late-night snowstorm some winters ago, he walked until he found an off-duty taxi. The sympathetic driver was nice enough to interrupt his coffee break and take Brown home. Brown didn't simply acknowledge the extra effort in the cabbie's tip. He offered him a job as a driver. Today, that driver is a marketing specialist.

"I like to see people and meet the public," says Brown. "By chatting with the taxi driver I found out he was a graduate of Amherst College and didn't have any plans." Brown also makes it a rule to forgo the self-serve pump at gas stations. Unpinched pennies at the pump have rewarded him with one especially courteous attendant who was ready to come in from the cold.

44

A Home Away From Home

When push comes to shove in a tight labor market, recruiting farther afield is certainly an option, but how much farther afield? If you want the new recruits to stick around, John Leehman recommends that you **look in "areas where the climate is similar to yours and the market is depressed**."

Leehman, executive vice-president of Bread Loaf Construction Co. - a 160-person business in Middlebury, Vt., in the heart of New England's ski region - considered both Denver and Houston as possible recruitment sites since the construction market was flat in both cities. Because Houston's climate differed so dramatically from Vermont's, Leehman ultimately decided to place a newspaper advertisement in ski-happy Denver.

It worked. Resumes flooded Bread Loaf's mailbox. Leehman spent two days in Denver interviewing approximately 30 candidates. Ultimately, he hired four employees.

In the ensuing two years, one did leave after his first six months and another eventually yearned for home and returned to Denver, but, Leehman insists, "For the cost of a hotel room, plane ticket, and 30% of their relocation costs, it was worth it."

Testing the Waters

Even the best interviewers sometimes make hiring mistakes, and those mistakes can be painful to admit, for both the employer and the employee. On the other hand, they can be even more painful to ignore. "It costs us a lot of money to make a mistake," says Doug Hard of Hard Engineering Inc., in Huntsville, Ala., "and it's tough on the employee, too. We have an environment geared to very high performance. You simply won't last if you can't keep up."

Hoping to alleviate the pain all around, Hard instituted a **90-day trial period for new employees** at Hard Engineering. By formal agreement, the company can terminate a new hire within the first 90 days if the relationship is not working out. The policy does not make it easy to fire someone, but it does remove some of the sting. "It allows you to say, 'Hey, it's just not a good fit,'" notes Jim Duggan, vice-president of marketing and sales, who recently had to say that to a new hire in quality control. "We pride ourselves on being a human company, and it's very difficult for us to do something that's perceived as horrible to an individual. This makes it more cut-and-dried."

46

Clinching the Deal

When recruiting top people, don't make the common mistake of assuming you can clinch the deal by adding a few thousand dollars to your offer. Money doesn't talk nearly as loudly as it used to, notes Peter K. Lemke, president of EFL Associates, an executive-search firm in Overland Park, Kans. More important may be factors such as club memberships, or help in relocation. The **trick is to figure out what the candidate really wants** - the "dealmaker."

Lemke advises that you approach the candidate as you would an important new customer, taking care to "read the buying signals." That means finding out everything you can about a candidate - from the ages of his kids to the work status of his spouse. Then be prepared to respond. "You can't afford to be rigid, not when you're trying to hire talented people," he says. "If you can't put the horse in the barn, someone else will."

TRAINING

"Ten years ago when we introduced
advanced training, people told us
they thought it was punishment
to have to come to the office and learn.
Recently we had them vote
on all our benefits, and they voted the
training program number one."

JOHN MCCORMACK,
chairman, Visible Changes Inc.

Reading Lists

"I don't have time to read all the **trade magazines** and keep up with technology," says Clay Page, CEO of Co-op Building Consultants, in Corpus Christi, Tex. But he doesn't let them pile up. Instead, at his residential construction company, he assigns masons to read up on the latest bricklaying techniques, carpenters to study stories about the newest saws, and framers to evaluate articles on aluminum versus wooden two-by-fours.

The reading helps employees keep in touch with what's going on beyond the job site. "These employees are helping to manage the company," says Page, who reads only what employees clip from the magazines. In 1989 Co-op's 54 employees improved productivity 220% and reached $2.7 million in sales.

48

Field Work

Putting new executives to work on the shop floor is a good way to bring field workers closer to the home office. But don't stop with your managers, says Jack Daugherty, CEO of Cash America Investments Inc., a $100-million chain of pawnshops based in Fort Worth.

At Cash America, **employees - from secretaries to accountants to the president - spend time in a store** getting familiar with systems for appraising goods, assessing borrowing needs, and writing loans.

That way, when pawnshop clerks or field managers call the home office, they don't get the runaround. After her stint behind the counter, Vicki Stanley, Daugherty's secretary, saw how merchandise was handled. Now if a clerk calls and has a question, she can help.

READER'S CHOICE

49

Book of the Month Club

What with all the daily newspapers, weekly magazines, and trade journals you have to read, odds are you don't have time to read the books that might help you - or your employees - run your business.

Alison Davis, who runs a public-relations firm in Hackensack, N.J., has a potential solution: **book reports**.

Once a month, an employee of Davis, Hays & Co. talks about a book he or she has read. "We don't assign books," says Davis. "The book just has to be related somehow to our business, and you have to give an old-fashioned, sixth-grade book report. You tell us what the book was about, what was interesting, and what you learned that would help us."

The company pays for the books, employees can read them on company time, and the book reports are given during office hours.

The reports have an added benefit, says Davis. "Since we go before the group and use overhead projectors and charts, it helps us work on our presentation skills."

Learn First, Pay Later

New, more efficient equipment is great, but it won't help your company until your employees have learned how to use it.

Quebecor America Inc.'s president and CEO John T. Collins has found a way to **guarantee that the vendor's trainer, as well as his own managers and operators, work quickly to get the new machines on-line** and the employees completely trained to run them. He withholds full payment until his operators confirm that they are 100% ready to go.

In addition to ensuring that the trainer works fast and well, the Needham, Mass., printing company's strategy ensures that employees take responsibility for fully understanding the equipment they'll be expected to make productive.

"It's as much psychological motivation as it is training," Collins says. "There's pride on the part of the employees when they tell their managers that they're ready to go. Consequently, they're much more motivated to do the job well."

Training Camps

One of the best ways to make job training bearable is to make it fun. What's more, a **training period that's enjoyable can foster camaraderie and introduce newcomers to a corporate culture**. Ask Joe Crugnale, who claims to accomplish all of the above every time he opens a Bertucci's restaurant.

Since 1985, CEO Crugnale's company, based in Woburn, Mass., has opened eight eateries, with five more coming soon. For the first two weeks of each launch, he and his top seven corporate managers work side by side with the waiters, bartenders, and dishwashers. After the weeks of tedious paperwork and negotiations, Crugnale claims, the prospect of manual labor is actually appealing. "We kid around a lot with the new hires, and it breaks up the monotony of the legal stuff for the managers. It's the fun part of opening a restaurant."

Managers of the new restaurants love the arrangement. "We know they need help, so we just fill in wherever we can for 15 hours a day," Crugnale says. Then there's the message it sends to employees: "The new hires see us go, go, go, and they work a little harder."

52

Getting Up to Speed Fast

What's the best way to break in a new executive? Put him to work on the shop floor. If you ask Henry Nasella, he'll tell you few experiences can match it for letting a manager see the company's problems firsthand.

Nasella had been a supermarket executive for two decades when he became president of Staples Inc., a $200-million chain of 40 discount office-supply stores with headquarters in Newton, Mass. He knew nothing about the office-supply business, so he spent a couple of weeks of his first month on the floor of one store, unloading delivery trucks, stocking shelves, and working the cash registers.

"I got a good handle on what we did well and didn't do well," says Nasella. "The things we didn't do well came through loud and clear."

When he took over operating responsibility a week later, Nasella was up to speed on how the business worked - a process, he says, that would have taken many months if he had stayed in the office.

Learning From Your Peers

Most CEOs would say their companies don't train and orient new employees as well as they'd like - including, until last year, Sally Tassani. Her solution? The buddy system. Each new hire at Tassani Communications Inc., Tassani's Chicago advertising and public-relations firm, is **paired with a veteran employee at a similar job level**, usually from another department. The buddy answers questions, makes introductions, and assays the ins and outs of Tassani corporate culture.

"We were frustrated that we weren't providing adequate job training, especially when going through fast growth," says president and founder Tassani. "New people really need someone they can go to and say, 'This is what they said, but I don't understand.' When the buddy is a peer from another department, new employees aren't as inhibited about asking questions."

New employees usually avail themselves of their buddy for a couple of months. "It's a great way to get everybody in the company involved with training," Tassani adds. "And it doesn't take a lot of any one person's time or money."

54

Finding the Right Seminar

Forget business seminars. For better information in your area of interest, **go to the sessions where experts inform the professionals in the field**. They aren't trying to sell anything, the presentation is more sophisticated, and you make great contacts in the bargain.

Cecil Ursprung, president and CEO of Reflexite Corp., in New Britain, Conn., wanted information on employee stock-ownership plans. So he attended a seminar designed for accountants and lawyers who administer ESOPs. "We went to hear the experts whom professionals rely upon," he says. "The information was presented in an unbiased manner, and they discussed the positives and negatives. We were much better prepared to evaluate our own lawyer's and accountant's advice." And when Reflexite's board voted to set up an ESOP, Ursprung had in hand a list of the best lawyers and accountants to hire for the transition.

Report Your Findings

To keep training dollars at work **after an employee returns from a seminar or conference**, consider having the employee give a mini-seminar afterward. It's a great way to make employees follow up on what they learn, reports Linda Miles, CEO of Linda L. Miles & Associates, in Virginia Beach, Va., which stages more than 100 seminars for dental-office staffs a year.

After staff members return from seminars, they report at a departmental meeting the three most important things they learned. The reports even make cross-training easier. "After our shipping clerk went to a postal-service seminar, all 20 of our employees learned how complex his job was and were more cooperative when changes came about," says Miles.

Home Movies

Contrary to popular opinion, training videos don't have to be expensive to produce or a drag to watch. Just ask the truckers at Motor Cargo, in Salt Lake City. There, a team of eight truckers and a dispatcher produced **an entertaining, informative video for their co-workers** on a tedious topic: how to catch billing errors due to inaccurate shipment descriptions.

Employees knew better than anyone what work habits needed sprucing up and viewed producing a video as a welcome break from routine, reports Kevin Avery, employee-involvement coordinator for the 700-employee, $45-million freight company.

The team of truckers donated 400 work hours to produce, direct, and act out scenes of billing mistakes. Motor Cargo paid $1,500 for the editing. The payoff: in a test study, $16.48 per bill was saved because of more accurate descriptions, and checking took only five minutes. "It's like a home video for the company," says Avery. "It's the first training video I've seen people excited to watch."

57

Training at the Top

In order to operate with minimum bureaucracy, you need managers who have the ability to function on their own. For that reason, Wilfred Olschewski holds **monthly management training sessions** for the managers at APEX Microtechnology Corp., in Tucson.

In one recent session, for example, a consultant focused on the art of hiring. "Everybody had been doing it differently and inefficiently," says Olschewski. "The consultant taught people how to get information out of applicants without getting too personal." The same consultant coached salespeople on the use of body language. "That sort of thing comes naturally to some people, but not to others. I figured it could only help make everybody more observant."

In the future, Olschewski plans to bring in an accountant for a session on reading financial statements - "It's something you have to know to be a good all-around manager" - and other experts will follow. At less than $200 for each 45-minute session, the program, he figures, is a bargain.

Keeping Up With Growth

No company can grow quickly unless its employees grow with it. So if you're hoping for rapid expansion, you should make sure that your **managers are training their replacements right now**.

Marjory Williams does just that at Laura Caspari/SHE, the chain of clothing stores she founded in 1979. Salespeople are trained by store managers, who are trained by area supervisors, who are trained by district managers. As a result, the company has a steady supply of managers available at all levels of the organization. The system has allowed Laura Caspari/SHE to grow to 18 stores in seven states and the District of Columbia, adding 8 new stores in one recent 12-month period.

The system works, says Williams, because everybody understands the thinking that lies behind it. "I let managers know that their jobs are not threatened by their deputies. People are rewarded by helping others to succeed."

59

"You've got to give people
a voice in their jobs. You've got to
give them a piece of the action
and a chance to excel.
You've got to give them the
freedom to have fun."

MIKE CUDAHY,
president, Marquette Electronics Inc.

Blowing Your Own Horn

S tarting a new business can be a pretty lonely endeavor. For one thing, there's nobody around to spur you on - or to give you a pat on the back when things go well. Back in 1981 Max Carey, CEO of Corporate Resource Development Inc., was frustrated by what seemed to him the slow progress of building his Atlanta-based sales- and marketing-services company. He had just one part-time employee, and "big successes were too far into the future," he says. "There wasn't much to motivate us."

His solution? "We decided to **celebrate the small interim successes**."

Carey went out and bought a siren, complete with megaphone and ambulance sound effects. After making a phone sales pitch, he would blow the horn if he had been able to bypass a training director and had reached a CEO. If a big check came in the mail, off went the siren. Now, the $1-million-plus company has 11 employees - and the siren goes off about 10 times a week. People come out of their offices to hear co-workers brag about their latest achievements, which helps companywide communications as well. "And it's a great motivator for our less experienced employees," Carey says, "who aren't yet able to produce at top levels."

READER'S CHOICE

60

Instant Gratification

When handing out bonuses for extra or exemplary effort, it may be timing, not quantity, that matters most. William T. Quinn Jr., whose W. T. Quinn Inc. ranked #128 on the 1987 INC. 500 list of the fastest-growing companies in America, has found that **his motivational dollars go further if he hands them out on the spot**, just when the work load "gets really crazy." Employees at the Somerset, N.J., publishing company don't get a chance to doubt whether the boss is grateful for their extra effort. And morale is buttressed right at the moment when employees are most stressed.

"The dollar amount of the bonus," Quinn says, "takes a backseat to timing." He hands out what he calls Quinn Cash, mock $50 bills with his picture on the front and a note that reads, "Redeem this with an expense voucher for $50 worth of entertainment." Why require that the money be spent on fun? "I want my employees to go out and have a good time," Quinn says. "It helps relieve job stress - saving up bonuses for a television set wouldn't do that."

61

Stamp of Acknowledgement

In the press of a busy day, it's difficult for most CEOs to keep in close touch with employees. Harry Seifert, CEO of Winter Gardens Salad Co., a 140-employee salad-manufacturing company in New Oxford, Pa., developed a simple, if slightly impersonal feedback system. He **rubber-stamps "Read by Harry" on reports** and routes them back to key employees for safekeeping. Time permitting, he augments the stamped acknowledgement with comments in the margins.

"For an employee, the worst thing is to be ignored," says Seifert. "Imagine if you spent all this time working on a report and it got stuffed in a drawer. It would really get to you. That's when quality slips." Since he began using the stamp a year ago, Seifert says the quality of the reports he gets has improved.

Preventing Burn-Out

"All you have to do is answer customer-support phones for two hours to realize how stressful it is and how important those reps are to building customer loyalty," says Don Emery, president and CEO of $5.2-million Reference Software International in San Francisco, a maker of grammar-checking programs. Fearful that his staff would burn out, he **set aside one day a week for customer service reps to work on self-designed projects**.

"It went over like a raise and has benefited our company as much as it did the employees," he says.

One employee programmed a demonstration disk that the company would have had to hire an outsider to do. Another started in-house software-training classes. A third started a computer bulletin board for grammar aficionados. The quality work at bargain prices and low departmental turnover offset the cost of hiring an additional rep to cover the phone lines, reports Emery.

63

Workers Anonymous

Production workers can often feel anonymous and under-appreciated, especially since they usually don't have their own offices. "It's crucial to break that barrier," says Chet Giermak, CEO of Eriez Magnetics, a $50-million manufacturer of magnetic laboratory equipment in Erie, Pa. "It's important that they understand that we need them."

That's why his factory has **nameplates in its work areas**. Each employee's name is engraved into a 4-by-30-inch slat, with the job description preceded by the word "sales" - as in sales/welding, or sales/machine shop - to reinforce the message that they play a key role in the company's growth. "I have a nameplate on my desk," says Giermak. "And these people are every bit as important to the company as I am.

"People like to see their names up there," adds Giermak. "Everybody wants to feel needed and useful."

64

Here's My Card

It's an old but true bromide: employees who are proud of what they do make better workers. Here's another easy way managers can help instill that feeling: make sure **everyone has personalized business cards**.

"A batch of cards costs us only $20," says Nancy Vetrone, president of Cleveland-based Original Copy Centers Inc., "and it's a hell of a simple way to recognize each person as important." Vetrone hand-delivers the cards to new employees within a week of their joining the company - a gesture that welcomes them to the permanent team.

The cards are also a cheap method of marketing, she says. "We've put 94 times more cards out in the world through our 94 employees. You never know who your people know."

65

Incentives That Don't Work

If you want to boost worker productivity, don't make the common mistake of handing out "recognition awards" to one or two of your star employees in hopes that others will take the hint and follow their example. It doesn't work. "To improve productivity, you have to foster teamwork," notes Bonnie Donovan of the American Productivity Center, "and **singling out the superstars tends to undermine team spirit**. If you really want to improve performance, then the rewards have to go to anyone who attains a given level of performance, and that level should be within reach of a lot of people."

This doesn't mean that recognition awards serve no useful purpose. You can use them to create role models and to give employees a sense of the company's priorities - provided you use objective, clearly defined criteria. Most companies don't. As a result, "people don't know what they have to do to receive [a recognition award]," says Donovan. "You've set up a target that nobody knows how to aim at."

66

"It's like having people sit on tacks.
It's hard for them to think of anything else
while they're doing it."

DAVID MORGENTHALER,
managing partner, Morgenthaler Ventures,
on why the wrong compensation system can be destructive.

Keeping Them Down on the Farm

How do you keep your best salespeople from leaving to work for somebody else? Or get an independent rep to pay more attention to your line?

The answer, says Jeffrey S. Adler, is "silver handcuffs" - **a deferred bonus plan**. Adler, a vice-president of the Insurance Services Division of Mesirow Financial, a Chicago-based financial services firm, explains how it could work:

You set a specific goal this year for your salesperson, who is generating, say, $100,000 in sales annually. You tell him for each year his sales top $110,000, he'll get a bonus of $2,500 - but the bonus is only payable after he has stayed with the firm seven years. If the salesperson hits his quota each year during that time, the company will pay out a $17,500 bonus in seven years. If the rep leaves before that, the company would keep the money.

67

Peak-Time Pay

Businesses with uneven workloads often run the risk of overstaffing, getting through crunch periods by carrying too many full-time employees. One solution is "peak-time pay," essentially a **premium wage for regular part-time employees who work during periods when the full-time staff is overburdened**. Companies can usually afford the higher wage because they don't have to provide part-timers with benefits, notes Stuart J. Mahlin, the Cincinnati consultant who developed the concept. And the money helps attract better-qualified, more dependable workers.

That, at any rate, is what happened at United American Bank of Memphis. "We had people overworked in some areas and underworked in others," says Morgan Brookfield, executive vice-president. "Morale was bad, and tellers were making a lot of errors." Using peak-time pay, the bank reduced its full-time staff from 113 to 95 people and added 19 peak-time employees, while holding its payroll steady. As a result, it now spends less than its competitors on personnel, whereas before it spent more.

"The bank has grown and is more profitable," says Brookfield. "We've improved morale, lowered error rates and absenteeism, and enhanced our work force, without spending money."

Looking at the Big Picture

Small, growing companies usually can't pay their people as much as the large outfit down the street. And while employers know that insurance and the cost of other benefits are eating them alive, their employees rarely understand the true expense of keeping them on the payroll.

Doug Greene, CEO of New Hope Communications Inc. - a Boulder, Colo., company that publishes magazines for the natural-foods industry and economic development - makes sure his **employees know exactly what it costs to keep them on board**.

"We don't just tell a new employee she'll be making $25,000 a year," says Greene. "We say her total benefit package is $36,750, and then we explain that in addition to the $25,000, we are also paying $495 a month for her insurance, $25 for parking, and so on down the line."

Greene is convinced his disclosure makes it easier to control his costs. In giving her a raise, Greene might tell the employee her total compensation package is being hiked 11%, including a 4% raise in compensation and a 7% increase in benefits. That helps impress upon the employee some of the increases in insurance premiums New Hope has had to pay.

READER'S CHOICE

69

Weary Wanderers

Lou Pearlman, founder and CEO of Airship International Ltd., in New York City, had a problem. Eight of his company's 42 employees were living on the road eight months out of each year to operate the two blimps the company leases. And they were growing weary.

Pearlman **offered them raises and bonuses, but family, not income, was the issue**. So he proposed spending any raises and bonuses normally incurred over the next two years on extra personnel, so employees' travel time would be cut in half. The managers agreed to a 20-month salary freeze, which Pearlman estimates paid for the cost of hiring the new managers.

"Knowing they can get back to a normal, day-to-day life," says Pearlman, "everyone is more eager to do the things they set out to do."

A Piece of the Action

When one group of employees earns commissions while others in support positions are on salary at the same company, resentment is the likely result. Bill Byrne, founder and publisher of *Tri-State Neighbor*, a bi-weekly magazine in Sioux Falls, S.D., found a way to reduce the friction. Without taking incentives away from his advertising reps, he lets others share in increased revenues.

Byrne still pays his reps a 5% to 8% commission. But for the past two years he's also run a **commissionlike program for his five production and administrative employees**. For every ad page sold above a base level, they split $20. As the number of ads sold has increased, the monthly shares have grown to about $200 a person.

Before, Byrne says, production people groaned when ads came in late. "Now, you don't hear those complaints. If anything, they're pushing the salespeople to get out and sell more." And because they want their shares to grow, they're less interested in adding new people to staff.

Bonuses for One and All

Most companies wouldn't think of **paying bonuses to part-time workers**. But Bulk International, which relies on high school students and other part-timers to staff its 25 company-owned retail stores, includes everyone in its bonus program. "The level of customer service can have a huge impact on what people buy," says Tom Cavalli, vice-president and CFO. "So employees are given an incentive to go that extra mile."

The company, located in Troy, Mich., sets monthly sales goals for individual stores during holiday seasons. If the target is met or surpassed, part-time employees can earn anywhere from 50¢ to $1 an hour on top of the $4 to $5 an hour they're guaranteed. Bulk International began offering the bonuses a year ago in hopes of generating more sales volume.

It's succeeded, notes Cavalli. "And one of the great things about this is that it's self-funding."

Making the Grade

To motivate student employees, Stuart Carey, owner of a Sonic Drive-In Restaurant franchise in Tucson, developed a simple bonus plan based on their grade-point averages. If a student works at Carey's fast-food restaurant for a whole semester and earns a 2.5 to 3.0 GPA, Carey awards a 15¢-per-hour bonus for hours worked that semester. He ups the ante to 25¢ per hour for students earning better than a 3.0 average.

The cost has been marginal: Carey spent $1,200 for the most recent semester, less than 5% of payroll costs for that time period. Each of the 18 employees who were eligible for the GPA bonus got one. "The hardest part is, they are the best students, so they get better opportunities and move on," says Carey.

But he's had no problem attracting replacements. The system so impresses a Tucson high school's counselors that they recommend students apply for jobs at Sonic Drive-In.

"We used to call them
'fringe benefits', but we quit using
the term 'fringe'
when we saw the magnitude
of that figure."

JAMES MORRIS,
director of survey research,
U.S. Chamber of Commerce.

Focusing on the Company's Assets

G iven the diversity of the work force, and the proliferation of new benefits, it's almost impossible to keep everyone happy, no matter how hard you try. Nobody knows this better than Edward Link, president of Link-Allen & Associates Inc., in San Mateo, Calif., a firm that specializes in marketing employee-benefit programs to other companies. What's critical, says Link, is to **take care of your key people** - a piece of advice that he follows at his own company.

At the beginning of every year, Link spends several hours in private with each of the five or six employees he can least afford to lose. During these meetings, he asks the person what he or she really needs. It may be extra life insurance, tax-deferred income, or a new car. In one case, the employee just wanted more time with the boss. "I try to focus on them," says Link, "and try not to superimpose what *I'd* like them to have."

Link says he couldn't afford to do this with all 52 of his employees, but he feels he has to try to accommodate his top performers. "You can't treat everyone equally, because they're not producing equally. But if I lose a key person, it will take at least a year for the business to recover."

74

Giving Employees a Lecture

W ant to score points with employees and keep them in tip-top shape? At $25-million Tassani Communications Inc., a Chicago advertising agency, employees can attend Food for Thought brown-bag lunches and listen to **lectures on such topics as stress management, crime prevention, and time management**. Says CEO Sally Tassani, "People enjoy topics that help them in their everyday life - things we tend to neglect when working long hours."

Tassani says attendance is better at irregularly scheduled lunches, which provide a break from routine, and when employees help choose topics. "For a couple hundred dollars per speaker, it's an inexpensive way to make this a fun place to work and learn," she says.

75

A Smorgasbord of Choices

Not every employee wants the same benefits package. Instead of medical or life insurance, some employees, especially those who are covered elsewhere, prefer cash.

So Judi Jaskiel, founder and CEO of JasTech Inc., a $6-million Cleveland computer-services business, **gives her employees a choice between two compensation programs** - a complete set of benefits and a salary; or a cafeteria plan, from which they can choose benefits, share the cost with the company, and receive a premium rate of about $28 an hour, about 30% higher than what salaried people get.

Once a year everyone gets the opportunity to reconsider. "If we only offered one of the options," Jaskiel notes, "I don't think we'd be as attractive to new employees. And we'd probably lose some of the people we have."

76

Giving Employees the Key to the Store

Fostering employee loyalty is a tall order for a CEO. One old-fashioned gesture of trust is giving employees keys to the store. At Edson International, in New Bedford, Mass., president Will Keene has given 7 of the 25 workers keys to the family-owned machine shop, which makes steering systems for yachts.

"These people have been with the company at least five years," says Keene. "They've made it known they plan to stay with our company for the long haul. They aren't out to rip us off." Newer employees get the message that long-term commitment is rewarded.

And the keys are used. **Employees can work on their own projects in the shop on weekends**, as long as someone else is present in case of injury. For workers who can't afford their own shop, it means a lot.

Avoiding the Company Car Trap

Don't let recruiting pressures force you into a hasty decision to provide your sales and service people with company cars. "It's a trap," says Stephen Albano, founder and president of Offtech Inc., a fast-growing (zero to $25 million in five years) distributor of office equipment based in Malden, Mass. "Once you start buying cars, you can't get out of it."

Instead, Albano pays each of his 64 salespeople and 140 technicians a flat fee, plus 10¢ a mile, for on-the-job use of their own cars. "We could have 250 cars in a fleet," he says. "Then we'd have to have a staff to run things" - not to mention maintenance and insurance.

Albano admits that his **no-car policy** is a disadvantage in recruiting, but he finds he can get around it by "walking [job candidates] through the logic." Most of them, he says, would prefer to choose their own cars, rather than drive a model selected by the department. The system also eliminates one potential source of bad morale - the used company car. "How would you feel if, your first day on the job, you got stuck with a 45,000-mile company car that needs new tires and has a rip in the seat?"

Solving Absentee Problems

One of a start-up's greatest luxuries is the freedom employees have to regulate the time they take off for sick days, personal days, and vacations. With a small, dedicated staff, peer pressure alone tends to limit the danger that the freedom will be abused. But what do you do when the company grows and abuses begin to crop up? Most companies feel compelled to start policing employees. But Gary Mokotoff, president of Data Universal Corp., in Teaneck, N.J., **has come up with an alternative, which he calls flex-leave**.

Under Mokotoff's system, each of the company's 35 employees is allowed six weeks off with pay during a year. That includes two weeks for vacation, 10 holidays, and 10 days for other reasons - sickness, death in the family, personal needs, whatever. "Every day you don't come in is counted toward the six weeks," says Mokotoff. If employees use less than the entire six weeks, they get paid for the balance in the form of a good attendance bonus. In practice, the average employee takes off a little more than five weeks per year, and the bonuses add up to about 80% of a week's payroll.

The policy has eliminated abuses of sick time, says Mokotoff, and ended controversy over holidays such as Good Friday and Rosh Hashanah.

When No Benefits Make Sense

Many a well-meaning employer has come up with a generous benefit package in the belief that it will tie employees to the company - only to find that turnover remains as high as ever. That's what Ron Cardoos discovered at his first company, a chain of gourmet food stores in the Boston area. Despite offering hourly workers medical and life insurance, paid vacations, and sick pay, the business experienced turnover as high as 300% per year - normal for a retail operation but a pain in the neck nonetheless.

So two years ago, when Cardoos launched his second company, Barnstable Grocery Inc., near Hyannis, Mass., he tried something different. He **dropped all benefits** except a 20% employee discount, increased starting salaries, and began reviewing each employee's performance every three months, handing out generous raises along with heaps of praise. He also gave employees the opportunity to work a "reasonable" amount of overtime for extra cash. The result: turnover has dropped dramatically, and his employees have never seemed happier.

"Instead of giving people what I think they should have," says Cardoos, "I'm giving them what they really want - a bigger paycheck at the end of the week. And giving them what they want is what counts."

80

Deals on Wheels

Bose Corp., a $100-million manufacturer of audio equipment, keeps the benefits rolling. The company earns gratitude from employees by **getting them attractive deals on new cars and trucks**.

Bose, located in Framingham, Mass., is a supplier of auto stereo parts for Delco, the electronics division of General Motors Corp. Because of its close relationship with GM, Bose was able to convince a local GM dealer to sell Pontiacs, Cadillacs, and GMC trucks to Bose employees at dealer cost.

The car program is available to any of the company's 900 Boston-area employees, provided they have been with Bose for at least two years. "The program has been very well received," says Ron Tuxbury, corporate manager of compensation and benefits. Tuxbury says that Bose is now developing a plan with a local insurance company, whereby Bose will be able to offer employees auto insurance through payroll deductions. Bose, it seems, is determined to keep its people driven.

81

Investing for Performance

D on't make the common mistake of building a long vesting schedule into your company's retirement plan in hopes of discouraging employee turnover. You just may be successful - giving unmotivated employees a reason to hang on when they should be replaced.

One company that has avoided this pitfall is Sonalysts Inc., an operations-research firm in Waterford, Conn. Shortly after the company was founded in 1973, the company **instituted a pension plan with an exceptionally short vesting period** - 25% a year, up to 100% in four years. Thereafter, employees could take the money and run. Most haven't. "Our turnover is very low for our business," says Muriel Hinkle, president of the 300-employee firm. The program has helped the company attract top employees, she adds, and they stay because they like the work, not because they're waiting to collect their retirement benefits.

82

The Most Exclusive Club

Deciding who gets a piece of the action in any company is no easy task. When Jim Scott, CEO of Bulldog Industries Inc., a $9-million Atlanta moving business and plastics company, decided to **give key executives a cut of his company** four years ago, his selection process was not unlike the time-tested college fraternity system.

Scott makes it clear to executives when he recruits them that after the first year or so, a candidate may be voted into the equity pool by the other - now seven - stockholders. Those chosen must pay dearly for their 1% to 3% of stock. "We figure out how much money someone has got, and then set the price high enough so they really have to sacrifice if they're going to be part of the team," Scott explains.

If stockholders want to quit, they must cash in their chips, and book value price is not an option. "They get what they paid plus interest," says Scott. "The ones who stick with me until the end are the ones who will benefit."

Computer Friendly

If your employees use computers off the job, they'll probably use them better at work. Walter Kisling, CEO of Multiplex Co., a St. Louis manufacturer of refrigerated drink dispensers, **offers his staffers financing on their home computers** - without interest and at a substantial savings.

The deal, though a valuable benefit for employees and their families, costs Multiplex little. When Kisling buys equipment for Multiplex's office, he passes the bulk discount along to employees. They pay just 10% down and cover the balance with monthly installments deducted from their paychecks. They pay no interest. The only cost to Multiplex is the finance charge on the money it fronts them for the machines. Of the company's 40-odd office workers, 15 have already made purchases.

Kisling is convinced that the program not only improves technical skills inside the company, but also boosts employee morale.

84

Getting a Bigger Bang for the Buck

Impressing on employees the value of retirement benefits can seem like one of the all-time great managerial challenges. But not if you present the benefits as simply as you would a savings account, discovered Engineering Design & Sales (EDS) CEO and president Roy G. Gignac.

The Danville, Va., electronic design and manufacturing company now **issues each eligible employee an ersatz savings passbook for recording profit-sharing vitals**: the company's contributions and interest earned. "Most companies hand out certificates at the end of the year telling employees how much they've socked away," Gignac says. "It gets stuffed in a drawer and forgotten. I wanted my profit sharing to have a more immediate effect on my employees - to be a reason to stay with my company. And I wanted to make it easy for them to understand how much we're doing for them."

On the first Tuesday of every month, the EDS accounting department makes the appropriate entries, based on the previous month's profits. "Employees can see their hard work pay off on a monthly basis, which is much more rewarding than yearly. And they take a more active interest in the plan."

"The thing about incentive plans
is that people take notice.
[If you don't have the right objectives],
you can meet your goal - and run
yourself right out of business."

JIM BERNSTEIN,
CEO, General Health Inc.

Pick Your Preference

If you rely on incentives to direct your team's efforts, thinking up new and different prizes can become a job in itself. Not so for Kirk Malicki, president of Pegasus Personal Fitness Centres, in Dallas.

When new physical-fitness trainers sign on with his personal-training company, he asks them to make a list of rewards, ranging in value from $25 to $200, that they'd like to receive for reaching weekly and monthly goals.

Instead of commonplace prizes, his 15 employees have opted for rock-concert tickets, limousine rentals, and half days off. Thanks in part to the **customized incentives**, sales have more than doubled over the past five years. "They know what motivates them better than I do, so I just ask," says Malicki.

Distant Rewards, Distant Success

D istant goals and deferred rewards can result in disillusioned employees. That's why at Seattle's Pacific Supply Co., workers take their bonuses one day at a time.

Every day that the apartment-supply company books $5,500 in sales, all 11 employees receive an extra half hour's pay. If daily sales hit $15,000, everyone racks up another 6 hours' wages. The previous year's sales provide the basis for Pacific's bonus targets. Paid out once a month, the bonuses accrue daily and in a typical month amount to an extra 20 hours' salary for each employee.

Since Pacific **scrapped a monthly incentive program for a daily one** four years ago, sales have increased by more than half; turnover has plummeted to only one resignation in three years, and daily sales targets are hit four out of five days a week. And company president Michael Go says that because all employees share in the spoils, "instead of fostering individualism, we get teamwork."

87

You Earn It, You Keep It

Pat Kelly, CEO of Physician Sales & Service (PSS), in Jacksonville, Fla., wanted his medical-instruments salespeople to sell a load of examination tables within 60 days. So he gave them a sales incentive up front: **cellular phones that they'd keep only if they sold enough** tables. "Once they got used to the phones, I knew they wouldn't want to turn them back in," says Kelly, who had the phones installed while he was offering his sales force the challenge at a meeting.

Kelly wanted PSS's 70 salespeople to sell an average of one table apiece. So the deal was that each of the 12 sales offices would have to sell one $4,000 table for each salesperson in the office. If an office fell one table short, its salespeople would have to chip in and buy one phone. The sales force not only reached its goal of 70 tables but surpassed it; 105 were sold, with no returns.

Paying for Savings

A big problem with most **employee-suggestion systems** is that the financial rewards, if they exist at all, are unrelated to the value of the suggestions. Without much incentive to find better ways to do things, many employees lose interest in trying. Not so at Peavey Electronics Corp. The Meridian, Miss., company pays hourly workers 8% of the estimated first-year labor and materials savings that result from their ideas.

Peavey, which makes amplifiers and guitars, used to have a more conventional system, rewarding suggestions with $25 to $100 bonuses, vice-president Melia Peavey explains. Paying for savings instead, she says, generates more excitement.

For each suggestion, the company projects the savings in a cost study. Then it pays the employee his or her percentage up front - a minimum of $15, with no maximum. "We give them the benefit of the doubt," Peavey says.

Salaried workers aren't included in the program. "Saving money is part of their jobs," she says, "and we don't want supervisors competing with hourly employees."

In 1988 hourly workers earned a combined total of $43,857 for their ideas. The biggest check - $1,331 - went to a machinist who figured out how to reduce the amount of maple scrapped by the neck-carving machine.

Tackling Trucking Turnover

Long hauls over the same roads were wearing on veteran drivers at The Daniel Co. of Springfield, a $4.3-million-based trucking company. The routine was taking its toll on the company, too, with sliding efficiency, employee turnover, and rising costs.

"There wasn't enough of a challenge to be more efficient," says president Larry Daniel. So he told drivers that if they **cut their costs, they could keep the change**.

Daniel's drivers pocket the savings they rack up by shopping for cheaper fuel, finding shorter routes, and improving their mileage. Some truckers earn as much as $2,500 in annual bonuses. Turnover has been cut by 25% as a result. And with drivers logging fewer miles, Daniel's trucks suffer less wear and tear.

Prospecting Pays

A problem with paying salespeople fixed-rate commissions is that, with enough steady customers, they could get lazy. Content to service the customers they know, they may be less eager to sniff out prospects. Bill Bozeman, CEO of Delta Audio-Visual Security Inc., a $3-million company in New Orleans that sells alarm systems to businesses and institutions, found a solution. His salespeople, who normally earn a 4% to 12% commission, can **earn an extra 1% when they sell to first-time customers**. On a $50,000 installation, that's another $500.

It may not sound like a lot, Bozeman concedes. But the opportunity to earn a bit more has influenced how Delta salespeople - especially the younger ones - spend their time. In the two years since the incentive was established, new-customer sales have risen from 25% of revenues to more than 35%. "Once we have them," Bozeman says, "we're in strong position to convert them to regular customers."

Family Support

To help his salespeople reach their goals, Tony Frederick has found an effective way to get their spouses involved.

Frederick, CEO of FrederickSeal Inc., in Bedford, N.H., a marketer of industrial sealing devices, holds a party every January for his salesmen and their wives (Frederick's sales force is all male). There, he announces an expenses-paid December vacation for each couple that meets specific selling goals for the year. Last year the winners went to Acapulco; the destination this year is Aruba. Every month Frederick **sends report cards home to the spouses**, detailing how well their husbands are moving toward their goals.

The system, says Frederick, motivates the women to help out at home. It gives them added reason to be tolerant of their husbands' long hours, too. "A salesman can tell his wife he's doing great, but each month she really finds out," says Frederick.

The report card also keeps the reward squarely in view at all times. "Most people can't keep their eye on the target when it's so far away," Frederick says. "We make it more immediate."

A Bunch of Carrots is Better Than One

Incentive programs can be powerful productivity tools, but you won't get the most out of them if you're not careful about how they're designed. For one thing, as Mary Shanley has learned at The Telemarketing Co., in Chicago, your **employees need to believe the rewards are within reach**.

Shanley's first program gave each of her telemarketers an only one-in-32 chance of winning the weekly prize - discouraging odds. Then one of her supervisors threw out the individual competition and in its place created four eight-member teams, each shooting for the $50 lunch awarded to the Team of the Week. "Now, instead of only one person getting to the top, eight people do. That's a 25% chance of winning," says Shanley.

Not only has productivity risen 20% under the team arrangement, but Shanley credits the new incentive system with building morale and fostering teamwork. "It makes our telemarketers help one another out more and keep one another motivated," Shanley says.

93

Thanks in Advance

During busy times of the year, it's great to be able to count on employees to give 110%. Harry Seifert, CEO of Winter Gardens Salads, Co., cooked up a recipe for productivity that's hard to beat. He **gives them a bonus before the busiest time of year hits**.

Just before Memorial Day, when he has the largest demand for his New Oxford, Pa.-made coleslaw and potato salad, Seifert dishes out $50 to each of his 140 employees to whet their appetite for the work ahead. "When I give them the money, I tell them we are going for a record to give them something to shoot for," says Seifert.

"Because employees are trying to achieve a goal," he observes, "they don't feel like they are being taken advantage of during the intense week." Production for that week is 50% greater than bonus-free holidays.

Seifert reserves the bonus for special occasions. "It's like the 100-yard dash," he observes, "you can't expect employees to sprint year-round.

Listening to the Customers

"We want this to be a customer-service-driven organization," says Bill Wheeler, president and general manager of Cellular One, of Indianapolis. So he got his six phone installers to approve a simple bonus plan that accounts for more than 10% of their pay.

As part of the plan, **each time a customer commends an employee's work** - in a letter, in a survey, or to Wheeler in person - that employee receives $10. Each time a customer complains about an employee, $10 is deducted, and $20 is deducted every time a customer's vehicle is damaged.

"Installers really go out of their way for customers now," says Wheeler, who estimates damages to customers' vehicles have plummeted 70%, compliments have tripled, and sales have grown by 613% since the program was started three years ago.

95

Productivity Pays

Gain-sharing first took hold in manufacturing companies, where it was used to reward employees for increased productivity. However, it has proved effective in service firms as well, ranging from restaurants and doctors' offices to electrical contractors and advertising agencies - any company that can accurately measure its costs of production.

According to Bill Jackson, a Marion, Ind., gain-sharing consultant, service companies generally base their **gain-sharing programs** on labor costs as a percentage of sales. Whenever employees bring labor costs in below a target percentage, the savings are divided among them at predetermined time intervals, usually monthly.

Jackson's son Clif, for example, put in a gain-sharing plan at his Marion restaurant. Eighteen months later, the company was operating with fewer employees, yet showing increased sales. In that year the plan paid out $8,435 in bonus money to its 18 employees - the equivalent in some cases of a 10.6% pay raise. "We have a high school girl who wants to come in part-time and bus tables. I've asked my employees to tell me when to hire her," Jackson says. So far, he hasn't gotten the go-ahead.

At Creative Professional Services Inc. (CPS) in Woburn, Mass., a $4-million direct-mail advertising service firm, CPS paid out $40,000 to its 75 full- and part-time staff in the first nine months of its program. "Our employees were skeptical because the plan didn't pay for the first few months," says president John Bell. "But now our people are intimately involved. They give us feedback that helps us provide more service more profitably. And if we screw something up, they want to know why."

Keeping their Eyes on the Prize

Sales contests are designed to motivate the troops, but once salespeople feel they're out of the running for prizes, they won't work as hard. Network General Corp., a software company in Menlo Park, Calif., took this into account when it designed a major selling contest three years ago for its outside reps. "It worked out great," says George Comstock, vice-president for business development.

Instead of offering one prize, the company set different award levels. At one level, for example, winners received a Caribbean cruise for one person, at another level the same cruise for two. Midway through the contest, a third level was added: a trip for two to Tahiti.

Instead of employees becoming discouraged, "these guys were pulling all the way through," Comstock says, and about 30 people won trips. The prizes cost the company a lot of money, admits Comstock, "but it was worth it - the contest has more than paid for itself."

97

Paper Chase

In a fast-growing company, paperwork - and the people who handle it - is often neglected. Michael Barrist, founder of NCO Financial Systems Inc., a $1.5-million collection agency in Philadelphia, **initiated a bonus system for his data-entry clerks that has brought the paperwork problem under control**. Productivity has increased an average of 25%, which, Barrist says, saved him from hiring, training, and managing an additional clerk. And there has been no drop in quality.

For every day finished without a backlog, each of NCO's seven clerks gets a point; at month's end, $250, $200, and $150 prizes are awarded to the top three performers. To keep the rest of the staff's spirits up, NCO also has a random drawing for a $100 prize. "This is a business where usually everybody works to win some prize or contest except the clerks," Barrist says. "This way nobody feels left out of the fun."

A Double Bonus: Productivity & Quality

While piecework payment systems can go far toward boosting productivity, too many CEOs have seen them lower quality at the same time. Does that mean that piecework has to go?

Walter Riley, CEO of G.O.D. Inc., a Kearny, N.J., overnight express freight service, doesn't think so. Riley, whose business depends on speed, has kept his piecework program, but he has **added incentives that specifically encourage quality**.

Four years ago, Riley took his freight dock loaders off hourly wage scales and paid them for each shipment handled. Freight loss and breakage became epidemic. "All of a sudden, there were problems all over the place. This system just sped them up. The dock loaders thought, 'If there are mistakes, there are mistakes.'" So Riley changed the system: on top of the shipment rate, freight loaders get weekly bonuses of 25% of their total week's earning if all shipments go through with no breakage, misloading or short cartons. For a dock worker earning $600 per week, that means an additional $150. Some 85% of dock workers meet the weekly bonus requirements. Plus, dock loaders now double as critical quality checks throughout the whole freight-hauling operation, improving companywide productivity as well.

99

Different Profit Measures Produce Different Results

Incentive bonuses can help in **getting managers to focus on profit-ability, but make sure that you use the right measure**. Otherwise, you may inadvertently send the wrong signal to managers and miss out on important profit dollars.

Many companies tie incentive bonuses to gross profit margins. That's fine, provided you want managers to concentrate on selling products or services that return the greatest profit per dollar of sale. The downside is that they may neglect the easy, but low-margin, sale.

To avoid that pitfall, Mississippi Management Inc., which operates hotels and motels, gauges its managers' performance by tracking their gross profit per available room (the standard unit in the hotel business). If the company tracked gross margin instead of gross profit, managers would be encouraged to sell more rooms, which are high margin, and discouraged from making, say, additional restaurant sales.

"Those other sales may lower margins, but they add profit dollars," says MMI controller Mickey Brady. So if you want maximum profit, not maximum margins, give managers a performance measure that doesn't penalize them for picking up those extra profit dollars in low-margin sales. Gross profit per square foot, or per hour of operation, might do it in your business.

100

No Expiration Date

A vacation giveaway is a classic sales incentive, but sales-quota deadlines can encourage last-minute sales and produce more losers than winners. Frank Garofalo, founder of Numismatic Investments of New England, in Salem, N.H., has found a better way. At Numismatic, contestants take as long as they like to generate $50,000 of rare-coin sales, at which time an $800 **travel credit is awarded**.

Winners appreciate the flexibility of choosing when, where, and with whom they can spend their vacation. And the costs work out about the same as the luxury all-expenses-paid vacation normally awarded.

Since starting the incentive program three years ago, 30% of Garofalo's 2,000 sales representatives have collected. He claims his improved plan helps distinguish Numismatic from a slew of well-established competitors, all vying for the reps' attention.

"People spend so many hours working at their job that making the vacation hours is much more special, and they remember Numismatic in that light," says Garofalo. "You should see our postcard collection."

101

The Prize is Right

If your company's incentive program isn't producing results, the problem might be simpler than you think. You may be offering the wrong rewards, rewards that simply fail to motivate your employees.

Phil Roberts, president of Premier Ventures Inc., found that his 30-day employee-motivation contest was effective with employees only for the first week. "After that, they just ignored it," he says.

Finally, a disgruntled Roberts - whose company runs six Denver restaurants - asked employees what he could do to motivate them. The answers surprised him. Few, he found, were motivated by cash, and rarely were all employees interested in the same booty.

Now, Roberts constantly monitors employees' desires and **offers a changing menu of prizes** from which his employees can choose. It gets complicated, he admits, "but it's also kept us ahead of the competition."

Creating Incentives for Hourly Workers

A successful program for motivating hourly workers has been developed by a little ($3-million in annual sales, 75 employees) company in Ashland, Ore., called Parsons Pine Products Inc. The world's largest manufacturer of slats for louvered doors and shutters, Parsons's principal claim to fame is its **four-point plan for "positive reinforcement" of workers**. The plan includes:

*Safety pay. Each employee who goes a month without a lost-time accident receives a bonus equal to four hours' pay.

*Retro pay. The company divides among employees the money it saves when its workers' compensation premiums go down due to reduced accident rates.

*Well pay. Employees get no sick days. Instead, they receive monthly "well pay," equal to eight hours' wages, provided that they have been neither absent nor tardy.

*Profit pay. Parsons has a bonus pool, into which goes all the company's earnings above 4% after taxes. An employee's share is determined by multiplying the person's wages or salary times a job rating based on attendance, productivity, and leadership.

Today, the accident rate is 32% *below* the state average; turnover is minimal, and absenteeism and tardiness have dropped to almost nothing. But owner James W. Parsons admits that the program takes a firm hand to administer.

"One woman called to say that a tree had fallen, and she couldn't get her car out. She wanted me to make an exception. But if I did that, I'd be doing it all the time."

103

Keep Those Wagons Rollin'

Beyond providing commissions for salespeople, many chief executive officers assume that searching for effective employee incentives isn't worth the trouble. But James A. Poure's experience suggests otherwise. Poure, head of General Alum & Chemical Corp., in Toledo, has built an **incentive program for his company's truck drivers** - with enviable results.

Instead of compensating drivers on an hourly basis, he encourages efficiency by paying them a percentage of freight tariff rates, which vary according to the weight of the load, the distance, and other factors. Now, says Poure, it's up to the drivers to manage their time. Whether a trip takes four hours or eight, they earn the same amount. To discourage speeding and overweight loading, drivers are required to pay their own fines.

Poure calculates that General Alum now spends 15% less than it would pay for outside trucking, due to efficiency gains. Plus, it retains good drivers. The company's seven drivers, who still get paid vacations and medical coverage, earn 10% to 30% more than they'd earn on an hourly basis.

104

"If more CEOs had to go out
and sell their products, day in and
day out, they'd pay a lot more attention
to what they were making.
When you're out there selling,
there's no place to hide.
It's the acid test."

JIM KOCH,
CEO, The Boston Beer Co.

An Offer That's Hard to Refuse

"**If we can convince a customer to visit our place, we'll make the sale** about 90% of the time," says Jim Ake, CEO of $11-million Electronic Liquid Fillers Inc. (ELF), in LaPorte, Ind. So Ake encourages prospective buyers by subtracting the cost of one round-trip airline fare from the invoice if the customer places an order for ELF's bottling machinery, which costs from $8,000 to $70,000.

ELF gets about one visit a day from a prospective customer. To the 50% of ELF's customers that are small companies, the airfare offer can be a deciding factor on whether to fly out, while big-company customers don't even bother sending in tickets for reimbursement.

"When they see this company has meat on its bones and will be here to service the equipment, it means a lot," says Ake. "It's well worth the cost."

READER'S CHOICE

105

Sending Out the Experts

What better way to prove your commitment to customer service than to **send your back office, the people who do the hands-on work, off to visit customers to complement your sales force**? Shepard Poorman Communications Corp., a $32-million printing company in Indianapolis, routinely sends its typesetters out to meet the editors whose manuscripts they work with daily.

Why bother? "They may not be slick salespeople, but they can solve problems for customers who didn't even know the problems existed," says vice-president for quality Don Curtis. He doesn't keep numbers on how the added investment in travel has paid off, but says customers are grateful, operations are more efficient, and product quality has improved.

106

Stuck With The Goods

Making a huge sale is great. But joy turns to regret if your customer gets stuck with merchandise and never orders again. "We don't believe in onetime deals," says Emery Klein, CEO of Alaron Inc., a $33-million electronics importer and custom product designer. So the Troy, Mich., company **encourages customers to order less so their cash isn't locked up in inventory**.

"We advise them to buy conservatively, and if the promotion goes well, we tell them, 'We'll be here for you,'" says Klein. When stores run low on an item, they can depend on Alaron to meet their needs, with delivery in about 10 days. "I'm a hero if customers have sold out rather than overbought. In the long run we end up selling more."

107

Make Everyone A Salesperson

If you think of selling as the exclusive responsibility of your sales force, you're probably letting business opportunities slip by. After all, employees don't have to work in sales to be capable of spotting potential customers. But they may not be alert to opportunities, or tell you about them, unless you give them a reason to do so.

At Computer Specialists Inc., a $5-million computer-service company in Monroeville, Pa., **nonsales employees have a strong reason to pass along names of prospective customers**. If a prospect turns into an account, the employee receives a bonus of up to $1,000, depending on the value of the job. Over the past year, the program has generated around 75 leads, resulting in nine new accounts, at a company cost of around $7,000.

Incentives keep everyone focused, says president Warren Rodgers, who uses them in other areas as well. "We key in the things that allow us to grow," he says. "We can't afford to have 50 salespeople scouting around for new business. This way, everybody who works here is a salesperson."

108

Old, But Not Forgotten

I f you're looking for new business, **you may be ignoring one of your best potential sources: old customers**.

That's what Michigan-based Van Pelt Corp., a steel service center, discovered last summer. During a period of sluggish sales, one of the company's inside salesmen sifted through its computer files and came across hundreds of customers who hadn't placed orders in more than a year. He began phoning them and, in a few weeks, generated more than $25,000 a month in additional sales. When salesmen left the company, for example, their accounts often were not pursued as aggressively as they might have been. Now, the company calls old customers regularly as part of its sales program.

109

Double Duty: Sales And Product Development

It's not unusual for companies to get their best ideas for new products from salespeople, since they tend to be closest to customers. What's surprising is that so many companies leave it to chance. Not so General Alum & Chemical Corp., based in Holland, Ohio. There, salespeople **can earn almost double the standard commission by generating orders for new products from existing customers**. Moreover, the salesperson continues to collect the new-product commission if he or she gets transferred. "It's kind of like a royalty system," says president Jim Poure.

General Alum's program grew out of Poure's own experience as a salesman for a large midwestern chemical company. Even without special incentives, he had made a habit of identifying new business opportunities for his employer. So when he began looking for ways to generate new business for General Alum, he naturally thought of his sales force as a prime resource.

"In particular, we look for products that are too small for big companies to make themselves," he says. As a result of leads from salespeople, General Alum is now making products for Mallory Industries, Oakite Products, and Dow Chemical. The new products, he estimates, account for an additional half-million dollars in sales per year.

110

The Value of An Educated Customer

We all know the long-term value of an educated customer, but Ron Cardoos has found that **customer education can generate immediate sales**. One night a week, Cardoos teaches a cooking class at Barnstable Grocery, the gourmet and specialty foods store he owns in Hyannis, Mass. Up to 15 people pay $20 each to attend. Although Cardoos just breaks even on the fee, he figures that every two-hour class generates an additional $500 to $750 in revenues, since customers often buy the products he demonstrates.

Cardoos began the program a year and a half ago, offering free classes taught by local chefs and cooking instructors. Back then, he would attract as many as 100 people per session. Now that he charges a fee, he gets a lower turnout, but he feels the attendees are more serious about cooking - and buying. By teaching the classes himself, moreover, he has greater control over the products he showcases, and he establishes closer contact with customers.

"It's selling," he says, "but it doesn't come across that way. And it makes the store a place where you not only buy food, but also get service and an education."

Knowing Your Audience

The last thing you want to do is intimidate a prospect on a sales call, but whip out a business card with *CEO* or *president* printed on it, and that's just what's liable to happen, says Phil Pachulski, CEO of Prime Technology Inc., a $33-million distributor of machine tools based in Grand Rapids. So Pachulski **keeps titleless cards on hand** for just such occasions.

"If hands-on plant managers and shop engineers see my title, they don't see me as their equal anymore," says Pachulski. "They think I'm a big-shot office guy who doesn't know what's going on in the marketplace."

But when calling on big-company employees to whom organizational charts are important, Pachulski presents a business card with his title, and voila, instant rapport.

Why?

"Meeting with a CEO makes them feel more important," he says. Such thoughtfulness has helped place Prime Technology on the INC. 500 list twice since its founding in 1982.

A Hassle-Free Travel Schedule

How many times has it happened: you call on a customer who puts you off by asking you to return in a couple of weeks? Trouble is, in a couple of weeks you're working a territory 100 miles away.

Tony Frederick thinks he's solved that problem. Frederick, CEO of FrederickSeal, Inc., in Bedford, N.H., a marketer of industrial sealing devices, divides each of his salespeople's territories into nine geographic areas of roughly equal size. The key to Frederick's system is the **sequence of visits, which makes it easy for salespeople to revisit customers who ask them to come back in a few weeks**.

Every month each salesperson concentrates on three of the nine areas. During the first week they cover one area; week two, they travel to an area on the other side of their territory; week three, they return to an area adjacent to the first, completing any unfinished calls while crossing the territory; and during week four they service key accounts in all three areas. The process is repeated during the second and third months so that by the end of each quarter, the territory has been covered.

Taking Advantage of Customer's Bonus Plans

You know your product can save a prospective customer money. The customer's employees know they can earn a bonus for suggesting ways to cut costs at their companies. Why not tie the two together and work them into your sales pitch? Bob Malone, CEO of Compaction Technologies Inc., in Portland, Ore., has done just that. He hit on the idea when he answered a phone call from a prospective customer's employee who wanted to know how much money Compaction's hazardous-waste trash compactor would save his company over a year.

Malone figures that in about half of the selling situations where it's applicable, this **cost-savings sales pitch** helps things get going. "Most of the companies that have these programs are larger companies," he says, "and the savings can really add up."

114

All Expenses-Paid "Vacation"

While **trade shows** may be great for business, they can be disruptive for spouses left behind. Bring them along, says Jim Ake, CEO of Electronic Liquid Fillers Inc., an $11-million bottling machinery maker in LaPorte, Ind. The only string attached is that they work a few hours handing out brochures and answering questions.

Ake figures the typical $2,000 bill for a couple of temps to work the booth was about the same as airfare, room, and meal expenses for two spouses, who would have a much better grip on the business. So he asks for volunteers. "We like to keep the money inside the company family if it's possible," he reasons. "When you try to make their lives better, then they try to make the company better."

Untapped Sources

Looking for business in unusual places is an approach Sheldon Goldner has honed to a fine art. On a recent trip to the federal courthouse in Chicago, for example, he picked up two dozen fresh leads for his company, Mar-Cor Industries Inc., which recovers precious metals from photographic scrap. One of his competitors had filed for bankruptcy, and Goldner figured that the court documents would contain lists of debtors and creditors, including potential customers. He was right.

Goldner also dabbles in telemarketing - from his car phone. Often, he says, he will pass a truck bearing the name and telephone number of a company that sounds like a possible customer. He dials the number on the spot, identifies himself, and asks to speak with the company's president. "I tell him I just passed his truck, and I'm calling in to report," says Goldner. "The guy usually laughs and asks how the driver is doing. You know, 'Did he hit you?'" Then Goldner makes his sales pitch.

The Deskless Sales Force

Taking the first step is often the toughest part of selling - so tough, in fact, that salespeople will postpone it as long as they can. Jackie Kimzey could see that happening at ProNet Inc., a Richardson, Tex., provider of paging services to the health-care industry. **His salespeople simply spent too much time in the office instead of going out on sales calls**. So when the company had to move to new quarters in 1983, Kimzey designed the space with the salespeople in mind. In place of offices, desks, and file cabinets, he gave them a modest workroom with a couple of tables and a copier. "They are more than welcome to stop by and make a few phone calls," he says, "but we don't want them hanging around."

Kimzey says there's been little grumbling about the no-desk policy. "We've heard from some people who've been here a while and would like their own little space, but we won't do that."

117

Laughing All the Way to the Bank

Show prospects a good time, and you may improve your sales. That's what the people at Properties of America Inc. discovered, thanks to a harsh winter. Clients from the city were calling about properties in rural New England, but an unusually heavy snowfall made the land difficult to show. So chief executive officer Philip Grande suggested that his salespeople put the clients on snowshoes. It worked like a charm.

"People from the city would show up after a rough week and a long drive," says Grande, whose company is headquartered in Williamstown, Mass. "We'd provide them with snowshoes to use, and it really changed their mood. And that's exactly what we want. We have to get them in the mood of having fun."

In a similar fashion, the company conquered the blackfly season in the hills of New Hampshire. Realtors gave clients safari hats with netting. "The idea was to make people comfortable," says Grande. "It was a great selling tool."

118

"Keep the right goal in mind:
don't look for money, look for applause.
If you create something of value
the sales will come."

ROBERT RONSTADT,
CEO, Lord Publishing Inc.

Guaranteed Attention

How do you push an invisible product? That was the challenge facing ComponentGuard Inc., a Valhalla, N.Y., business that sells extended warranties for consumer electronic items.

CEO Robert Minnick came up with a novel approach: he put his service contract and membership card in a colorful plastic package that hangs from retail racks like a stereo accessory. With the new packaging, sales jumped to $6.1 million in 1990, from $1.4 million in 1989. In fact, sales for the first quarter in which the new package was used nearly equaled the revenues for all of 1989.

Sharing the Wealth

Competitors can be good for business, believes Richard Gsottschneider, CEO of RKG Associates Inc., a $1-million real estate consulting firm in Durham, N.H. He **gets job referrals by sending his company newsletter to his rivals**.

The semiannual four-page newsletter features items on RKG projects, regional news, and economic issues. It costs about $1 per newsletter to produce and mail to some 1,800 current and prospective clients and 200 competitors.

The first two mailings brought two jobs - and lots of leads from competitors, he says. "We refer work to them, and they do the same for us. There's more than enough work to go around."

Training Wheels

To CEO Bill Buckingham, "Going Mobile" is more than just a song by The Who. It's also a way to broaden his business base. His $2.9-million training and service company, Buckingham Computer Services Inc., recently hit the road with Training Wheels, a 34-foot motor home equipped with six personal computers and a VCR that plays training tapes.

The Midland, Mich.-based company has training labs in four states, but its largest customer - Dow Chemical Co. - operates nationwide. "We're **now able to take the training right to them**," Buckingham says. "We're now getting business that we'd otherwise lose."

The downside? "It takes some courage to drive that thing," he says. "It's so big."

Success Can Kill You

As many fast-growing companies discover, too much demand can be just as troublesome as too little. The challenge is to come up with a **strategy that slows the stampede for the understocked product**, but doesn't permanently extinguish its sales momentum.

Bruce Katz, president of The Rockport Co., a Marlboro, Mass., manufacturer of casual shoes, faced that dilemma when orders from retailers for his walking shoes poured in so fast that the company couldn't keep up with demand.

Concerned about alienating his market, Katz decided to try an unorthodox strategy. He suggested that retailers buy from competitors whose shoes are similar in price and style to Rockport's. "It hurts us to say, 'Buy from a rival,'" notes Jens Bang, the company's marketing vice-president. "But every time a shopper walks out the door, the retailer is going to miss a sale and hold us responsible."

The company has also placed a one-year moratorium on opening new accounts. In addition, Katz plans to provide continual updates on the company's progress: A recent letter to all retailers reported on Rockport's new computerized inventory system.

Finally, the company has begun to redirect its marketing and advertising to focus on available inventory and has also stopped advertising a toll-free number for shoppers who want to locate retailers who carry their products.

"It may be frustrating to pull back after gearing up," says Bang. "But retaining customer support will allow us to grow even more in the future."

Building Customer Loyalty

Chances are, your company could benefit from increased customer loyalty just as much as the airlines can. So why not borrow their most effective gimmick? That's what Terry Finn did when he **adapted the frequent-flyer idea** to One Hour Delivery Service Inc., the courier business he runs in Dallas.

Like the plans it mimics, Finn's frequent-caller program targets the actual users of his service. The secretaries, mail clerks, and receptionists who decide which courier will be summoned are the program's beneficiaries.

Customers accrue one point per delivery, except for downtown deliveries, which are only a tenth of a point. Monthly statements of point balances are accompanied by a four-color flier promoting such popular prizes as chocolates (30 points) and a dozen roses (15 points). "We're putting a lot into this program," says Finn, whose clientele has stampeded to sign up, "but customer loyalty is worth it."

READER'S CHOICE

123

Finding a Responsive Environment

Richard A. Gagne, owner of Dental Horizons, in Oxnard, Calif., never used to be sure which of the many places he advertised were generating the most dollars of dental service. Then he started listing different phone numbers - his office has several lines - in any advertisements that were running concurrently.

"Now, we always **track which ads are drawing phone calls**," says Gagne, who compares response rates to ads in different publications, and then allocates his ad budget accordingly.

Forgo The Logo

Forget bulls and doughboys - what do you have as your corporate logo? If you answered "nothing," you may be better off, says Bill Drenttel. His company, Drenttel Doyle Partners, is a New York City advertising and design agency that develops corporate identities and logos. Growing companies shouldn't waste a lot of time trying to create a symbol they can call their own, he says. "As more and more big companies go about creating - or recreating - their logos, you're bound to get lost in the clutter," Drenttel adds. "Your **best bet is to let your product's name stand for your company**." It works for companies from Oshkosh and Smuckers to Marriott.

125

Promotional Values

Giving discounts or including a free gift with a purchase is a sure way to increase sales - but only if the deal is worth what you say it is. "Nothing turns off the consumer faster than saying you are giving them a $9.95 value, when they know they can go down to K mart and buy the same thing for $5," says Clifford Medney, director of sales promotion for A&W Brands Inc.

But you don't have to spend full price to give someone a true bargain. A&W, for example, purchases thousands of teddy bears in the Far East, knowing similar bears retail for $25. By going directly to the manufacturer, A&W can pass its discounts on to customers. A&W is happy because the $9.95 that consumers pay for the A&W Great Root Bear covers expenses. Consumers are happy because they save more than 60%.

If It Ain't Broke, It's an Asset

I n need of a fresh competitive edge? Maybe your company already has one, and you just haven't looked for it hard enough. Take the case of Steve Rondel, president of $1.8-million Advanced Products & Technologies Inc.

Rondel was standing in the mail room of his Redmond, Wash., business when he realized that very few customers were returning the portable coffee makers, hair dryers, and other travel products he makes.

Then the light bulb went on. The **reliability of his company's products could be exploited**. Why not offer a five-year warranty as a way to differentiate Advanced Products from the pack? Given the low return rate, what could it cost?

Virtually nothing, as it turned out, and the payoff can be enormous, especially if yours is a higher-priced line. The warranty, says Rondel, tells consumers the product is worth it.

Constant Reminders

In a sea of competition, is it possible to remind former and prospective clients that you exist without constantly bugging them? Alan Gaynor, who runs a Manhattan architecture and interior design firm, thinks you can by **using cards to keep your work in their minds**.

Every time Alan Gaynor & Co. gets a new job or completes one, Gaynor sends out a wedding invitation-size card to 1,200 names on his mailing list. The card names the client and explains what the 21-person firm has been hired to do for it.

"The cards remind people we're still alive," says Gaynor. "What's more, a builder might learn that we also do interior work, or somebody who has used us on interiors can see we're capable of designing buildings.

"We try to do a mailing every two weeks," Gaynor continues. "It's like advertising - you have to keep sending out the message if you want it to sink in." With postage and printing, mailings cost around $500, but Gaynor says it's money well spent. "If we get one job every two years as a result, the mailings pay for themselves."

"Anyone who tells you
retailing is wonderful and exciting
is out of his mind."

DAVID LIEDERMAN,
CEO, David's Cookies

Homing Device to Track Customers

You spend an hour talking about the benefits of your product line, and then the **customer walks out before you have a chance to get his or her name and phone number**. Barry Fribush, founder of Bubbling Bath Spa & Tub Works, in Rockville, Md., says with his system, that'll never happen again.

"While we are making our sales pitch," explains Fribush, "we hand the customer a coupon that entitles him to $125 worth of merchandise if he buys from us. We tell him that because this is a special offer, we need to track every coupon, so we need his name, address, and phone number."

If the customer balks, "We say that's perfectly OK, but we need the coupon back." Fribush says in the seven years he has been giving out coupons - which are redeemable for a chemical kit, pillows, and extra filter cartridges - "maybe a handful have given it back. Once we have their names, we follow up forever."

A Picture is Worth a Thousand Words

Judy George, founder and CEO of Norwood, Mass.-based Domain home-furnishing stores, thinks a picture really is worth a thousand words in her business. Before potential customers leave one of Domain's 10 stores, they **get a Polaroid snapshot of the furniture they are considering**, and the salesperson writes his or her name on the back of the photo. The photo helps customers feel more comfortable choosing Domain's furniture, George believes, because they can compare it with products at other stores and their own home furnishings.

Customers are also more inclined to keep the snapshot - and thus remember the product and the salesperson's name - than a business card. "It helps them feel secure with the purchase; it bonds them with the salesperson," says George, who reports that the technique has increased Domain's sales-closing rate by about 25%.

READER'S CHOICE

130

When Less is More

Test-selling a product for possible addition to your line can be dangerous. If you add the item, you'll buy big quantities to get the best price. But if it doesn't move during your test, you can be stuck with an unsalable inventory. Which is why, says Stew Leonard, paying more is sometimes a better deal.

Before Leonard places a big order for a new item, he'll order a smaller lot and sell the item for less than he paid. "Sure I lose a little money, but I find out if it really is a good deal," says the Norwalk, Conn., retailer. "If I sell out, I'll buy the truckload. If I don't, I'm not stuck with something I can't sell."

It's a lesson he learned the hard way. "We were offered a truckload of shaving cream at 99¢ a can, or 10 cases at $1.39. I took the truckload because I was sure we'd sell out. We didn't. I initially priced it at $1.19. I finally sold it at 69¢, buy two get a third one free."

131

When a Product Doesn't Sell

Norman Melnick, chairman of Pentech International Inc., an Edison, N.J., maker of pens, pencils, and markers, is proud of his successful 50-product line. But occasionally even he produces an item no one wants to buy.

When that happens, Melnick does everything in his power to get the product off the shelves quickly. He gives the retailer a choice between accepting money that can be used to advertise the product or simply sending the product back at Pentech International's expense.

"If a product isn't selling, I **want to get it out of there because it's taking up space that can be devoted to another part of my line that moves**," says Melnick. "Besides, having a product languish on the shelves doesn't do much for our image."

PRICING

"I think it goes for any business that price differentiation requires product differentiation."

JAN CARLZON,
president/CEO, Scandanavian Airlines

When a Price Hike Makes Sense

Often small companies operating in a competitive industry will undervalue their goods or services - pricing them as if they were basic commodities rather than value-added products. The consequences can be life-threatening.

When a consultant suggested that Gordon Whitney raise his prices 20%, he was dumbfounded. "I thought it was suicide," recalls Whitney, president of G.J. Payne Co., a Santa Ana, Calif., asphalt recycler. But sales had fallen to $4 million from $6.2 million a year earlier and the company had registered its first unprofitable year in two decades.

That was two years ago. Payne now anticipates sales of about $6.5 million, and its pretax profit margins are 15%, up from 6%. Harry Dahlberg, a consultant with Durkee, Sharlit Associates in Los Angeles had reviewed Payne's financials. Payne's scenario was one Dahlberg sees all too often: a mature company in a competitive industry steadily lowering prices to maintain accounts, only to price itself out of business.

Dahlberg prescribed strong medicine. Payne's owner and president took pay cuts of 25%, while all other salaries fell by 15%. Regional offices were closed. But the cost-cutting measures still left the company far short of its cash goals. The only option left was to raise prices.

To Whitney's surprise, few customers balked as Payne levied price hikes totalling 20%. Even more surprising was that the competition quickly brought their prices in line with Payne's higher fees. "Our consultant explained that if we thought we were the quality company in the industry, then we should be the market leader on price".

133

Getting Priced Out of the Market

O ne of the most common mistakes of small exporters is to leave pricing in the hands of their overseas distributor or sales representative. In one recent survey of small to midsize technology companies, about half reported that they **had no idea what the markup was on their products sold abroad**. The danger is that prices set by a distributor or rep may not serve the interests of the manufacturer. "Maybe the rep carries American tools and Japanese tools," notes W. K. Schoonmaker, editor of *Mainly Marketing*, the Coram, N.Y., newsletter that conducted the survey. "He may get a bigger cut of the Japanese tools, so he may price the American tools to encourage sales of the Japanese line." For advice on pricing abroad and other aspects of exporting, contact the nearest field office of the U.S. Department of Commerce.

Avoiding the Price Cut Trap

Whenever sales get soft, you can bet that someone in your company will start pushing for a price cut. That's often a bad idea. A price cut may not generate enough new sales to make up for the loss in profitability per sales unit, especially when the market for your product is weak to begin with.

So how do you solve your sales problem without cutting prices? One way is to **bundle a couple of products together**, as Chuck Sussman of Pretty Neat Industries Inc. did when sales of his cosmetics organizer began to fall off. "I had already been planning to introduce a new version of the product, at about half the regular price," he recalls. "Instead, I priced the cheaper model at about 90%, shrink-wrapped the two products into one package, and stuck on a Day-Glo banner that said, 'Free $4 Value with This Purchase!' They sold like crazy. Customers kept the expensive product and gave the inexpensive one as a gift. And, of course, we wound up increasing our margins, not cutting them - which is what would have happened if we'd cut prices."

Sweetening the Deal

Many a vendor combats price resistance by offering reluctant customers a little loan. The tactic can enhance sales, all right, but it generates collection problems as well. An alternative is to **come up with a second product** that, when sold with the first, makes the combined package too good to pass up.

That was the strategy developed by Al Burger, founder of "Bugs" Burger Bug Killers Inc., the Miami-based exterminator company noted for its effectiveness in banishing creepy creatures from restaurants and other institutions. Problem was, its standard fee was so out of line with the competition that many restaurants chose to forgo Burger's pest-elimination measures in favor of cheaper, if shorter-term, options.

So Burger came up with a second service. For an additional fee, his pest eliminators will also clean refrigerator coils, reset seals, and otherwise help restaurants control their energy costs. Annual cash savings to the restaurant in many cases covers the cost of pest elimination - not to mention the fact that regular maintenance may prolong a refrigerator's life by a cool 600%. The catch is that, in order to get the energy service, customers have to sign up for pest elimination, too.

"When you're fighting the war
with limited resources and no track record,
it's tough. You can easily wind up
where we did:
on the bottom shelf, in back,
behind the pole."

KEN MYERS,
president, Smartfoods Inc.

Providing an Incentive for Third Party Sales

If you depend on third parties for sales, you want to give them reasons for moving your product. That may mean **helping them to market themselves while they are selling for you**.

John McCormack had that goal in mind when he introduced the Brocato line of hair-care products, to be sold through hair salons. The chairman of Visible Changes Inc., a Houston-based chain of salons, McCormack knew how important it was for a hair-cutting establishment to keep its name in front of customers. He thought, why not design his products for that very purpose? So he left a space on each bottle where the selling salon could affix a sticker with its name and telephone number. Not only that, but he arranged to provide the salons with stickers for about 4¢ apiece.

In five months, more than $700,000 worth of the product has been sold through about 2,000 independent salons around the country.

READER'S CHOICE

137

Take Down My Number

Effective distribution is tough for any new consumer-product company. So when Elizabeth Andrews, CEO of The Baby Bag Co., in Cumberland, Maine, began selling her innovative infant outerwear, she **made sure buyers could find her even if they couldn't find a store that carried her goods**. She stitched her new company's address and phone number right on every Baby Bag's label.

It seems to have worked. Though Baby Bag had difficulty winning shelf space from retailers, potential customers who saw the products being used at the grocery store or on the street were often intrigued enough to ask about them. Once they had the number, they could call Andrews to place an order or learn where the company's items were available for sale.

"Later, when Baby Bag became better known, retailers objected to the number because they thought it would take business away from them," Andrews says. Now that distribution is good, each Baby Bag has the company's address but not its phone number.

"We still get plenty of calls from customers in rural regions who are serious enough about wanting one that they dial information to get the number. And the 800 retailers love it because they get referrals."

138

Greasing the Skids for Distributors

If you have just one product in a distributor's catalog, there's a good chance the product isn't getting the attention you think it deserves. At $3.8-million Delta Technology International Inc., a software business in Eau Claire, Wis., CEO Jim Anthony **supplements his dealer-distributor network with four of his own salespeople**, who lay the groundwork for a sale and then turn over the closing and commissions to Anthony's local distributor.

"Selling these customers takes an average of two to four months, and distributors don't want to invest that amount of time in us," says Anthony. "But when our distributors make a little easy money thanks to the supplemental sales effort, it reminds them that our product does sell, and then they sell more of it themselves."

One closing can pay for a salesperson's annual base salary, says Anthony. The bottom line? Delta's product ranked in the top 20 of an industry best-seller list for 1989, and Anthony is hiring another corporate salesperson.

139

"Smaller companies really are
in a catch-22 situation.
They can least afford to pay for
information . . . but they need
the research more
[than the *Fortune* 500 firms]."

JOSEPH SMITH,
president, Oxtoby-Smith Inc.

Taking Stock of Competitors

If you compete against a publicly traded company, don't overlook the opportunity you have to gain insight into your competitor's operation, financing, and strategy. All it costs is the price of a share of the competitor's stock.

Last spring, Jim Pierson **bought some shares in a publicly traded competitor** that had begun showing up in markets served by his company, J. W. Pierson Co., an East Orange, N.J., wholesaler and retailer of petroleum products. "I wanted to keep track of what he was doing," says Pierson, "and the best way was to read his shareholder reports."

The investment has paid off, he says. "I can actually see where he gets his money, and I now have a good idea about his cost structure and acquisition plans." Not that the information has forced Pierson to alter his own plans. "Mostly it's broadened my perspective and given me new clues to work with. Based on my reading of his costs, for example, I don't think he's in a position to cut his prices. And that's just fine with me."

Free-Trial Feedback

Looking for another source of cheap and on-target market research? Donald L. Beaver Jr., founder and chairman of New Pig Corp., has found one: **disgruntled not-quite customers**. He calls them not-quite because though they use his products, they decide not to pay for them.

Here's how Beaver's plan works. To sell prospects on the Altoona, Pa., company's "pigs" - devices that absorb leaks around manufacturing machinery - he offers 20-day, no-risk trials. If you don't like the pigs, you can ignore the bill. When a bill is ignored, Beaver calls to find out why. The result? Ideas for new or improved products. One customer, for instance, said he wasn't paying because his pig reacted with the nitric-acid leaks it was absorbing. Beaver explained that the product hadn't been designed to deal with hazardous fluids - and set about developing one that could. Today, he says, the resulting hazardous-materials pig is a $2-million-a-year product.

The key to the strategy, Beaver says, is the ignore-the-bill offer. Without it, dissatisfied customers would pay up the first time but never order again, and their immediate feedback would be lost.

Share and Share Alike

Chances are, **outside your selling territory, companies like yours are just as hungry for marketplace information as you are**. They aren't your competition, so why not share secrets? That's what Sheila West, CEO of Archery Center International Inc. (ACI) in Monroe, Mich., figured when she bought an archery retail shop full of bows and arrows she knew nothing about. "I didn't know who else to call and I needed to know what to order for the upcoming season," admits West, who now runs $3.4-million ACI, an archery equipment distributorship spun off from the retail shop.

Early on, store owners were suspicious of her motives, and hang-ups were common. So she offered them the phone number of a manufacturer who would vouch for her. She conducted short interviews with about 20 shop owners and got a handle on which products were hot sellers, the best quality, and good prospects for the upcoming season. "People who warmed up to the idea found they wanted to know about these things just as much as I did," says West.

READER'S CHOICE

142

Tracking the Trends

In an age of instant communications and fast-moving markets, it isn't easy for retailers and wholesalers to keep up with customers. By the time you get the products they want, they've often moved on to something else. Granted, you can try to stay ahead of them by closely monitoring the trends in your business. But that takes time and money - especially if you're located far from industry centers.

Such was the challenge facing Buster Simon, owner of a women's apparel store in Stillwater, Okla. His solution: **hire a representative** in New York City to keep him abreast of the latest fashions and hottest designers. Simon says he spends much less on the agent's fee than he used to spend on buying trips to the Big Apple. And the arrangement has given him an important competitive advantage. "I'm often the only one in my part of the country carrying certain lines," he says. "I don't think I could do it on my own."

"Finding the right agent [in a foreign market] can be only slightly easier than finding the right marriage partner. "

OTTO NEDELKOVICH,
vice-president, Autosplice Inc.

Cooking Up Sales

When you're selling to a foreign prospect, the pomp and circumstance of formal meetings may get in the way of closing a deal. After 20 years of selling internationally, Wayne Cooper decided to **balance the formality with an evening of casual entertaining**.

It began when Cooper, CEO of 13-year-old Arcon Manufacturing Inc., in Charlotte, N.C., invited a delegation from China over to his ranch to cook its favorite dishes. "They had been on the road for a month and missed their native cuisine," explains Cooper, who then sold them a grain-storage system the next day after a year and a half of meetings.

To keep things simple, the five- to six-person delegations just cook for themselves, Cooper, and his wife, Judy. Business is not discussed. "In meetings prior to the dinner, they feel like you are trying to pull one over on them and are suspicious; afterward they want my advice," claims Cooper, who now turns his kitchen over to visiting chefs once a month.

READER'S CHOICE

144

World Piece

Lining up good stateside distributors is challenge enough, but **finding committed distributors overseas** is even more daunting. Most foreign distributors will want exclusivity. Should you grant it?

Yes - and no, says Roy Kessler, president of PC Globe Inc., a $6-million Tempe, Ariz., company that put the atlas onto software.

At first Kessler cut a deal offering exclusivity without any performance clause and with no insistence on a front-end order. Overseas product sales languished.

Now if distributors want exclusivity, Kessler offers 20% of what they think they can sell in a year as their first order, which must be prepaid. "They don't get an exclusive so much as the *opportunity* for an exclusive," says Kessler. As long as they keep ordering as much as their first order each quarter, they retain their monopolies. To date, PC Globe's German distributor has maintained its exclusive rights. The product sells in 15 foreign countries, accounting for 15% to 20% of overall sales.

What Are Friends For?

Whiat with the constant influx of foreign competition, and the falling dollar, you'd love to beef up your company's presence overseas. But the idea of setting up foreign distribution, hiring a new sales force, and trying to keep an eye on performance "over there" scares you to death. What to do?

Think like Michael Lepiner. The president of Los Angeles-based Telecom Entertainment Inc. has come up with a way to make international business less daunting: **find a foreign friend, and have him buy in**.

Telecom makes television movies - such as *The Attic: The Hiding of Anne Frank*, - but Lepiner's approach could work for almost anyone. When developing a movie script with international appeal, Lepiner searches for overseas broadcasters and offers them a piece of the action. In return, he gets more than money - he gains knowledgeable foreign contacts and help with distribution, production, and advertising. There is no need for brokers or other middlemen.

Although in most cases the arrangement works like a joint venture, Telecom often retains the final say, which can be part of the deal's appeal. Also appealing is the potential for reciprocity. Says Lepiner: "When your foreign partners are looking to do business here, they're likely to come to you."

146

Scouting Out Foreign Markets

Murray Shields, vice-president at ADM Technology Inc., a manufacturer of media production equipment, was asked a year ago to head up the Troy, Mich.-based company's export initiative. Using government programs and research, Shields has **set up an exporting network of agents** that now brings in 30% of ADM's $5 million annual sales.

Shields started at the U.S. Department of Commerce offices in Detroit, where he submitted a description of the kind of agent he needed to represent his company abroad. Using a list of names collected by Commerce officials through consulates and embassies overseas, Shields requested World Trade Data Reports on each, including information on a candidate's customers, bank references, estimated sales volume, and assets. He then narrowed it down to three agents per country. It wasn't always difficult. In Korea, for example, one agent handled farm animals and feed in addition to electronics. Shields crossed him off the list. He next visited the final candidates in person. "I asked each agent to introduce me to some of his customers to see what the relationship was like."

Shields initiated other contacts by asking U.S. manufacturers in his industry that make noncompetitive products for the names of their agents. In addition, he scanned trade magazines that list overseas agents, contacting the most promising ones.

The key is keeping in touch, Shields says. He spends about five months a year traveling overseas. "You must be seen continuously by these people to say, 'Remember us.' They may not have sold anything for you since you saw them last, but you want them to keep trying."

MAILINGS

"We write
the catalog copy as if
we were writing a letter
to a friend."

NORA GALLAGHER,
editor, Patagonia Inc. catalog

Going Directly to the Source

I f you're trying to market a product by direct mail, it's important to send your promotional pieces to people who both appreciate its value and have the ability to buy it. That's particularly true when you're selling to businesses, and so many companies direct their pitches to people relatively high up the corporate ladder - plant managers, chief financial officers, presidents, and the like. But **sometimes it pays to go a few steps down the ladder**.

The New Pig Corp., for example, figured that janitors were the most likely purchasers of its new device for absorbing oil leaks around manufacturing equipment. Unlike the plant manager, a janitor would immediately comprehend the product's benefits and might well have the authority to make a $100 purchase. Besides, president Don Beaver figured, janitors don't get much mail.

So Beaver rented a list from the American Institute of Plant Engineers and mailed letters to the "facilities manager" (rather than the engineers) of plants on the list. "What we were trying to do," says Beaver, "was get to the guy pushing the broom." The mailing produced 295 orders, generating 188 new clients, and got Pig's marketing program off to an auspicious start.

Cleaning the List of Deadweight

I f you market by direct mail, you'd probably love to: (1) identify who reads your material, and (2) drop the prospects who never even open your brochure. Doug Hotchkiss, sales and marketing director of Overseas Adventure Travel Inc. (OAT), in Cambridge, Mass., thinks he has a way to do both.

Last year OAT **included a high-stakes contest in its mailing**. In order to know about a trip to an exotic locale that the company was giving away - you could choose, say, Nepal or Peru - you had to at least open the six-page brochure. And in order to enter the contest, you had to answer six questions drawn from the brochure's text: for example, "Which nonfamily trip is the least difficult of our treks in Nepal?"

The trip cost the company as little as $1,800, Hotchkiss says, an insignificant expense compared with the $112,000 in printing and postage OAT saved by cleaning its mailing list of deadweight. Even better, those who entered the contest also had to answer questions about where they wanted to go and when: perfect fodder for OAT's salespeople.

The Winning Ticket

We've all received direct mail promising unbelievable prizes inside, only to be disappointed when we opened it and found a hitch. However, one hitchless contest that's on the up and up and needs no explaining is a state-run lottery.

Andy Juster and Scott Pilato, cofounders of $2-million-a-year Sunny Waterbeds & Accessories Inc., located in Orlando, decided to make good marketing use of their state lottery's credibility. They **stuffed lottery tickets into mailings** they sent to their top 100 retailers to announce a new line of bedroom furniture. The mailings specified when Sunny Waterbeds would follow up with a call. "Lottery ticket enclosed" was printed on the envelope.

The net result? When Sunny Waterbeds called a week later to announce the winning number, 70% of the prospects took the call and listened to its pitch. Usually 15% take the follow-up call on a mailing. "We were surprised," says Juster. "You wouldn't expect these people, who are really important, to hold on to a $1 lottery ticket for a week."

READER'S CHOICE

150

Don't Be Duped

If you sell by direct mail and are **acquiring new mailing lists**, make sure that the names you're getting aren't ones you already have. "It's gotten to be a very incestuous world out there," says Gordon Segal, whose company, Crate & Barrel, has been mailing out catalogs for about 10 years. In the early days, he says, he didn't worry much about duplication between lists. "The overlap between lists you had and lists you bought was maybe 10% to 15%." Lately, however, the dupe rate has risen to more than 30%. "Everyone is looking at the same people," says Segal.

So before you shell out money for new names and addresses, you'd be wise to test the lists for overlaps. Otherwise, you may get less than you pay for.

Sending Just a Teaser

A picture is worth 1,000 words or, more accurately, $23,000, says Saul Rowen, executive director of Cali-Camp Summer Day Camp, in Topanga, Calif.

To cut costs, Rowen, instead of sending out 16-page brochures that cost 72¢ apiece to produce and mail, **now sends just the brochure cover** along with photos of camp life and a response card that can be sent in to request a complete brochure. At a cost of 43¢ a package, this practice saves 40% of the cost of brochures.

"We're saving money, and we're hitting our exact market," says Rowen, whose mailing to 46,000 prospects yielded 23 new campers worth $1,000 a head.

"We're little; they're IBM.
We had to be faster. There are only
two kinds of people who dance
with elephants - the quick
and the dead."

MARK CUBAN,

*president, MicroSolutions Inc., a company whose responsiveness convinced
Neiman Marcus to buy IBM PCs from them rather than IBM itself.*

Most Valuable Players

While baseball fans cheer at the World Series, American Information Systems customers will be fielding fly balls batted by AIS employees. Seven years ago AIS was a Fort Lauderdale, Fla., start-up eager to build customer loyalty for its integrated telephone and computer systems. CEO Jack Namer found baseball to be the ticket.

Today each of AIS's 61 offices has **sold customers on a 10-month-season baseball program** playing against AIS-employee and other customer teams. The top teams play off in a championship series at the New York Yankees' spring-training field in Fort Lauderdale. AIS, a $15-million company, picks up the tab for the weekend series. "If they switch vendors, our customers have to turn in their uniforms," says Namer. "They're loyal."

Watching Dough Rise

Lots of managers chatter away about the importance of keeping customers satisfied. But Frank Meeks, CEO and owner of Domino's Pizza Team Washington Inc., which owns 42 stores in the Washington, D.C., area, thinks employees have difficulty committing themselves to abstractions. So he spells it out for them.

Employees are taught the dollar consequences of alienating customers. "Many customers," Meeks explains, "do business with the company twice a week, spending close to $1,000 annually, not including tips. Extending that over seven years, that's $7,000. And unhappy customers tell about a dozen other people, multiplying the potential damage even further."

All problems don't disappear by educating people about those numbers, says Meeks. But it does help them focus on the importance of happy customers. "We want them to adopt a philosophy about what they do. Having a number helps us do it."

154

Expert Advice

Your **line employees could be some of the best salespeople you have**. After all, who knows the product better than the folks who make it?

When J. W. Kisling, CEO of $26-million Multiplex Co., in Ballwin, Mo., gives tours of the beverage dispenser manufacturing facility, he stops by a workstation and asks one of the company's 120 factory employees, "How about explaining to us what you're working on?"

Why? "It impresses a customer to see our employees are able to explain what's going on around them. Everybody's a salesman here." It's difficult to measure how much business this tack brings in, but with customer comments like "These guys really know what they are doing," Kisling's sure it hasn't hurt revenues one iota.

Jumping the Gun for the Customers

Sometimes even your guaranteed service falls short. The job then, according to G.O.D. (Guaranteed Overnight Delivery) Inc. CEO Walter Riley is to turn that minus into a plus. G.O.D. **doesn't just offer a money-back guarantee - it sends customers their refunds even before they ask for them**.

The Kearny, N.J., overnight express-freight company sends the accounting department an invoice, but it sends the purchasing agent a report detailing the previous month's deliveries and dates missed (if any) and a refund check made out to purchasing. Why not deal just with accounting? "Because the people who pay the bills don't decide who to use," Riley says. "This kind of itemized report really impresses purchasers, who 99% of the time don't even know they should get money back. A record and check is relatively simple for us to generate but would be a hassle for them. And they look better upstairs."

The policy not only provides Riley's salespeople with more ammo, but it reminds purchasing agents that G.O.D. is an *overnight* delivery service - unlike most other freight services. And it keeps company performance statistics rigorously up to date, enabling Riley to take the pulse of G.O.D. at any given moment.

156

Minimizing Double Trouble

Some customers just seem to attract problems. "It's like a restaurant," says Neil Cannon, chief executive officer of Schmidt-Cannon Inc., a distributor of promotional items in City of Industry, Calif. "The guy who gets the cold soup also gets the hamburger that's well-done when he asked for rare."

In an effort to minimize cases of double trouble, the staff **developed a system for tracking orders from customers with past problems**. Whenever the company receives a complaint, that customer's next order is placed in a red file folder to alert the staff to take extra care. When the folder passes through each department, the manager signs off on it personally. Later, if a problem arises, he or she talks directly with the account.

Since the system was introduced three years ago, the incidence of repeat complaints has dropped noticeably, says Cannon, who notes that Schmidt-Cannon processes about 6,000 orders per month. "Often, you get a repeat because it's a problem customer. We do everything we can to make sure they're happy. This way, we can be pretty positive that we've done our job."

157

Talking to the Silent Minority

There are customers out there who are simply afraid to complain - who'd rather switch companies than fight. The problem is, that can wreak havoc on repeat business and word-of-mouth advertising.

Clarke Otten, president of Professional Swedish Car Repair, in Atlanta, **ferrets out nonconfrontational customers by telephoning all customers one week after they visit** either of his two locations. He sets aside an hour or two a day to make 20 to 50 calls.

Customers remember that the president of the $1-million company called them and really feel serviced. And, "I can get them to admit what's bothering them and address the problem right on the spot," he says. The calls also keep his 12 employees on their toes. "They know I'm in touch with the front line and know better than to try to slip anything by," Otten says.

158

Get What You Pay For

Few companies these days fail to recognize the importance of offering great customer service, but that doesn't mean you have to give it away. Karmak Software Inc., in Carlinville, Ill., **abandoned an old-style service policy for one that asks customers to pay more if they want more support** - and the switch has worked.

Under the old plan, a fixed customer-service charge was tacked onto every sale. Customers treated the add-on as just another component in the software price, and didn't hesitate to call on Karmak's service department as if its time were free. Service costs, says CEO Richard Schein, began wrecking the company's bottom line. "Instead of using the manuals or actually learning the system, people would call us with every itty-bitty problem. And we were paying for it because we guaranteed unlimited consultation after the sale."

Now, customers must sign up in advance for the level of service they want - a set number of calls per month and a surcharge for calls in excess of the contracted number.

"If a customer wants us to answer a simple question that could have been looked up in the manual, or if he has such high turnover that we have to go in and train people again and again, it's not a problem," says Schein. "They're paying for it, not us anymore."

Schein won't say how profitable customer service has become, but he claims, "It's so great we doubled the size of the department."

159

Giving Credit Where Credit's Due

Customers can be a good source of new product ideas, but if you don't acknowledge their contributions, you may be missing out on a chance to win their loyalty, as well as their business. One company in Cleveland goes so far as to **award plaques to customers who offer suggestions leading to new products**.

The company, Crescent Metal Products Inc., manufactures and distributes equipment for the food-service industry. About two years ago, a food-service director of the San Diego schools approached Crescent with an idea for a mobile serving table for the school yard, offering students an alternative to their usual fast-food diet. Crescent went on to produce the table, which last year was one of the company's top 25 products out of 800 overall.

In appreciation, company president George E. Baggott presented the food service director with a plaque and publicized her contribution in the company newsletter and the trade press. He has since done the same for other customers, thus encouraging new ideas and winning a few points in the process.

160

You Oughta Be In Pictures

Want to get a customer's attention? When prospective customers visit Eriez Magnetics, a $50-million manufacturer of magnetic laboratory and metal detection equipment, the receptionist **lines them up underneath a sign with the company trademark on it and snaps their pictures**. "It's just our way of saying thank you," says Chet Giermak, president and chief executive officer. "We're complimented you'd come all the way to Erie, Pa., just to see us."

The photos have a more practical purpose as well. Giermak sends them to visitors complete with a cover letter reminding them of their reason for coming and the people they met. He slips the photo into a cardboard frame with the company's mission statement on the back. "It's a little memento," says Giermak. "Sometimes, after getting it, potential customers will let us have a second crack at them."

Giermak says that it takes only a minute to dictate the letter and that each complete package costs about $2, including the stamp. "Most people like to have their picture taken," he adds. "It makes them feel important."

READER'S CHOICE

161

Eliminating Surprises

Here's **one way to get employees to focus on customer service**: set specific, measurable goals, with rewards for achieving them. That's what Ed Loke did, and he's not only reduced his company's shipping errors by 75%, he's also improved employee morale.

Last August, Loke instituted a "No Surprises Guarantee Program" at Trelltex Inc., a $5-million, Houston-based industrial rubber products wholesaler. In a written statement to customers, he promised that Trelltex would ship goods within 24 hours, notify them of back-ordered items prior to shipping, ship the correct goods, and make no pricing errors. "If we fail you in these areas," he pledged, "we will mail you a check for $25 to help compensate for the inconvenience of our error." To cover the guarantee, Loke set aside $250 a month. "We told our order-handling people that if we made fewer than 10 errors, we would give them the balance of the $250 in cash."

The result: Trelltex went from making 10 shipping errors a month - each costing about $200, according to Loke - to a mere 2 or 3. "It has saved us a fortune," he says. Meanwhile, Trelltex has fewer dissatisfied customers, and more employees who are committed to customer service.

162

Making Your Customer Your Partner

Even if you've developed a wonderful retail consumer product and have positive results from focus groups and test markets, if buyers for the nation's retailers aren't convinced, you're never going to get on the shelf. Norman Melnick, chairman of Pentech International, a maker of inexpensive writing and drawing implements based in Edison, N.J., convinces the buyers by turning them into his partners.

Before going into production, Melnick **talks with the buyers and lets them shape the final product**. If they want his pens to come in a 16-pack as opposed to an 8-pack, he'll do it. They think the package takes up too much space on the shelf? No problem. The packaging will shrink. Buyers have become part of the manufacturing and marketing process and develop a vested interest in the product's success.

And Melnick, whose company now sells $23 million worth of products a year, makes them put their company's money where their advice is. "Pentech does not produce an item without an order in hand," he says.

163

Removing the Middle Man

Think twice before creating a system in which customers deal only with salespeople. Often you can provide better service - and run your company more efficiently - by **letting customers deal directly with the people who do the work**.

With that thought in mind, Hugh Vestal reorganized his small machine-tool business, Carbide Surface Co., in Frasier, Mich. Now, when a customer needs a tool coated with carbide, he talks with one of the five "impregnators" who actually do the coating. The impregnator schedules the job, arranges for delivery of the part, performs the work, and submits a job-cost form to Vestal. Customers like the system because it spares their having to work through intermediaries. Shop workers like it because it challenges them and breaks the monotony of the job. And salespeople like it because it frees them to focus on getting new business.

164

Spotting the Problem Customer or Vendor

I t's all well and good to develop friendly relationships with your customers and suppliers, but **don't shut your eyes to signs of trouble**. Some are fairly obvious, notes Douglas A. Phillips, a bankruptcy expert with the accounting firm of Weber, Lipshie & Co., in New York City - signals such as the departure of key employees, or inexplicable delays in shipments. Other warnings may be more subtle. In particular, Phillips suggests that you watch for:

*frequent changes in accountants or lawyers ("If it happens a lot, chance are it's more than a dispute over fees")

*unexpected sales of assets ("If the reason doesn't make sense, you should be asking questions")

*a shift in financing, say from using a bank line of credit to factoring of receivables ("It may not mean anything. Then again, it may be the smoke that leads you to the fire").

Of course, you can best determine how far to go with suppliers and customers by examining their latest financial statements, as certified by an accountant. You should ask for them. "If you think something's funny and the company doesn't want to provide adequate information," says Phillips, "then you should think twice about the terms you're offering."

The Personal Touch

The personal contact you have with customers is a crucial element in the success of any new business - and one of the most common casualties of growth. "As a company grows, the president tends to fade away into his office," observes Joseph Cherry, founder and president of Cherry Tire Service Inc., in Maybrook, N.Y. "He loses contact with customers" and thereby loses some of the leverage the company had when it was just starting up. The company can become just one more of the faceless entities a customer deals with every day.

That danger is even greater, Cherry realized, in an era when companies rely increasingly on computers to handle communications with customers. So he **instituted a simple policy of sending a personal thank-you note to each customer** of Cherry Tire. Now, every evening he sits down to sign a stack of cards printed with "Thank you" on the front and, inside, a message reading, "Thank you very much for calling Cherry Tire Service. We really appreciate the business."

"It's hard to keep up with, but it's worth it," says Cherry. "It's better than newspaper ads because each card goes right to the person I want to reach. And customers don't forget it."

166

The Customer Knows Best

Handling customer complaints can be a tough job, but one that plays a crucial role in your company's overall marketing success. So **how do you get employees to go the extra mile for complaining customers?** One way is to base a part of their compensation on customer evaluations of their performance.

Renex Corp., a manufacturer of computer peripherals in Woodbridge, Va., does just that with the 12 employees in its customer communications center. The marketing administrator contacts each customer who has called in with a problem and asks him or her a series of questions about the performance of the company and its customer service representatives. The administrator uses the answers to calculate a score for the employees who handled the problem. Each person's scores are then averaged quarterly, producing a rating that is used to determine the employee's quarterly bonus. That bonus may amount to as much as 25% of the employee's overall compensation.

Under the system, Renex's typical service rep winds up making about 10% more than the industry average. "It gives our technical support staff the drive to keep doing their best for customers," says Shane Clawson, director of sales and marketing.

Plugging His Customers

Advertisements are everywhere. And Dave West, vice-president of San Luis Sourdough, in San Luis Obispo, Calif., uses this trend to his advantage. He **runs ads in his company newsletter**. West could have found paying advertisers for his quarterly six- to eight-page publication, but he gives away the space, using the ads to plug his customers.

The ads are nothing fancy. They promote whatever the customer wants and, of course, mention that the customer carries West's bread. "It's another way to thank the people who do business with us," says West.

Mingling Customers and Employees

Among every chief executive officer's toughest challenges is keeping employees focused on what matters most - which, in the case of William H. Wilson's Pioneer/Eclipse, is "customers and quality." For Wilson, president of the cleaning-system manufacturer, instilling that focus was a two-step process.

First he initiated a "CQ" (customers and quality) campaign, handing out CQ badges, buttons, and posters, and placing CQ notes in pay envelopes. "The problem in my manufacturing plant was that employees didn't relate to customers," Wilson says. "They didn't realize that their boss is the customer."

To hammer home that lesson, Wilson puts his employees in closer contact with customers. He **rotates managers into the customer-relations department, where they deal with the people who use the company's products**. And he takes customers on tours of his plant, where they are introduced to line workers. The point, Wilson says, is simple: "We want to live and breathe the CQ program."

Are We Having Fun Yet?

"People don't even want to talk about accounting it's so boring," says Yvonne Angelo, cofounder and vice-president of SBT Corp., an accounting-software business in Sausalito, Calif. You need an ice-breaker, she says.

When Angelo's receptionist came to work dressed up for the Fourth of July and customers laughed or stopped to talk to her, Angelo knew she was on to something.

Not every day is a costume party, but Angelo now **gives employees at the front desk a stash of cash** to buy yo-yos, candy, and assorted toys. The result? Laudatory letters from customers spill in faster, she reports. "If employees are relaxed and having fun," Angelo explains, "it comes across to our dealers."

170

Just a Phone Call Away

Want to let your customer know how committed you are to serving them? For the past four years J. W. Kisling, CEO of Multiplex Inc., a St. Louis maker of beverage-dispensing equipment for the food-service industry, has listed the **home phone numbers of the company's 16 directors** and officers in its catalog. Next to the list is a suggestion to call in case of emergency - if satisfaction can't be had from an area manager. "The secret," Kisling confides, "is we only get a couple of calls a year. But seeing it in writing impresses the hell out of our customers."

171

Taking Orders

You labor long and hard to find customers, and what happens when they call up to give you an order? All the salespeople are at lunch or handling other calls or otherwise occupied. What do you do?

Gus Blythe, president of SecondWind Co., which sells athletic-shoe-care products, has the answer: **turn every employee into a potential order-taker**.

Blythe has order forms hanging from each desk in his Paso Robles, Calif., company. "That way, when the phone rings, we have no excuse not to take an order," he explains. "The forms are self-explanatory, and every employee, including me, is capable of filling them out. There's nothing worse than making a customer wait to give you money."

Capitalizing on Complaints

Most managers view customer complaints as annoying headaches. John Wirth sees them as opportunities. Not that he likes having dissatisfied customers. But some are inevitable, and he's found that they are well worth the time it takes to assuage them.

"A customer with a satisfactorily resolved problem will produce three times the revenue of a customer without a problem," says Wirth, president of Woodworker's Supply Inc., a mail-order company based in Albuquerque. "Down the road, when you and six other competitors reach his mailbox, your letter will stand out. The customer develops an affinity for you that he doesn't have for the others." And, Wirth adds, the customer will probably recommend you to friends.

So how do you resolve the customer's problem? "Let him sound off," says Wirth. "Then ask what he would like you to do. Ninety percent of the time he comes back with something reasonable - often less than you would volunteer to do yourself." To make sure that employees make the most of every such opportunity, Wirth conducts training sessions in which they handle simulated complaint calls.

173

Passing Ideas Along to Customers

Good ideas for serving customers have a way of slipping through the cracks. To prevent that from happening at his company, Mike Berthelot developed a simple form that accompanies each client's file as it makes the rounds of Berthelot & Associates, a Cleveland-based management-consulting and accounting firm. Called the **"pay-for-me" form**, it provides a space in which any employee can jot down suggestions on how the client can save money or increase income.

The form serves several purposes, says Berthelot. "In busy periods, it keeps the staff focused on doing what our clients hire us to do." It also helps ensure that good ideas aren't lost. "People are always coming up with ideas for clients but forgetting them in the press of business." Perhaps most important, the form gets the entire company thinking about customer service. "We want the clerical people involved, too."

And one other thing: clients love it. "When I tell prospective clients about the pay-for-me forms, they are thrilled."

"If you break the rules,

you're going to stand a better chance

of breaking through

the clutter . . . to disarm the consumer,

who increasingly has got

his defenses up against all sorts

of advertising messages

coming his way."

TOM MCELLIGOTT,

president, Fallon, McElligott agency

Bartering for Ad Space

Television commercials are expensive. So are newspaper ads. So what's the most cost-effective way to reach potential customers? For Stuart Skorman, president of Empire Video, the answer is to use other stores and businesses in the area to help get your message across.

Skorman, who runs Empire Video Superstore, a chain of five stores based in Keene, N.H., **swaps free and half-price movie-rental coupons to area merchants in return for advertising space in their stores**. Or he'll offer them advertising space in his stores or in his newsletter to his 17,000 customers. Each year the exchanges get 50,000 to 100,000 pieces of promotion per video store in customers' hands. "It would be hard not to find advertisements for our stores in any of the communities we're in," says Skorman.

175

Write on the Money

You want high visibility in your industry, but a full-page, four-color ad in a trade magazine can run about $4,000. Ron Harper, chairman of Harper Companies International, a $17-million holding company based in Charlotte, N.C., found a way to save money without sacrificing visibility.

Harper offered a $500 **bonus to any employee who could write a technical article** and get it published in a trade magazine. To date, at least 10 of his employees have met the challenge, which cost Harper $5,000 for what he guesses to be $40,000 worth of publicity. "Plus," he says, "the articles have a lot more credibility than an ad." To boost production, Harper lined up a local free-lance writer with whom employees can work and split the take. "Those who feel uncomfortable writing have no excuse now," he says.

176

Choosing a PR Firm

Thinking about hiring a public relations firm? Maybe you should check out its reputation with the reporters who cover your industry. "Reporters know better than anyone if we're good at our job," notes Sally Jackson, president of Jackson & Co., a Boston public relations firm. Reporters, after all, are on the receiving end of a PR agency's letters and calls. They know which firms they pay attention to, and which they ignore. And, they generally won't hesitate to tell you if the agency you're considering is one that makes them cringe. If so, ask for the name of a better, more credible publicist.

There's a secondary benefit to **calling reporters for references**: at the same time, you will be introducing them to your company, which probably won't hurt your future public relations efforts. And you may someday be glad that you have your own direct contacts with the media - in case your PR firm doesn't work out.

Broadcasting Your Credo

Smart managers never miss a chance to explain what their company stands for. Do you guarantee the lowest prices? Fastest service? Biggest selection? Why not **tell the world about it - right on the back of your business card**?

That's what Thomas L. Venable, chairman of Spectrum Control Inc., has done - and he claims that it has helped distinguish his firm from his competitors.

Venable places a 45-word message, entitled "Spectrum's Quality Response Process" on the back of each employee's business card. It stresses that the company is "committed to quality performance" and strives to do each job "error free."

"These goals are important to us," says Venable, whose Erie, Pa., company ensures that differing technological devices will work together.

He says the cost of adding the message is small, since 50,000 cards - each containing the company's name and address on the front and the message on the back - are printed at a time. The cards are then customized to include the employee's name, job title, and telephone number.

Buying the Generic Brand

When Rich Davis acquired an ailing Battle Creek, Mich., Buick dealership he decided to scrap the company's advertising campaign and fire the ad agency. But he quickly discovered that writing the ads himself was time consuming. So Davis decided to experiment with a different strategy: shared advertising.

Banks, jewelry stores, car dealerships, funeral homes, furniture stores - just about any local, retail-oriented business that provides a fairly standardized product or service - **can cut down on expensive production costs by using syndicated commercials**. These are, essentially, generic advertisements, developed for a particular type of business, with local information dubbed in.

Clients find that good syndicators can offer significant savings, and often high-quality work. "We'd get great service from our [local] agency the first year; mediocre the second; and lousy service the third," says Robert Wilkie, of the Newport, N.H., Sugar River Savings Bank, which signed on this year with Leon Shaffer Golnick, a Ft. Lauderdale, Fla., syndicator. He claims that his bank's radio ads now stand out from those of his competitors, many of which have the local radio station dee-jays read the ad copy. Moreover, Sugar River will be able to double its media budget by eliminating the high production costs charged for advertising by its agency.

Two words of caution: Avoid syndicators whose campaigns show little understanding of your industry and your customers' needs. Also, before using syndicated advertising, get a contract specifying that the agency will not sell the same campaign to other companies in, or near, your marketing area.

179

Educating Your Market

Good marketing often takes the form of education, but few companies go about it as intelligently as Computer Specialists Inc., a fast-growing computer-service business in Monroeville, Pa. Two or three times a year, the **company sponsors "executive briefings"** at a local country club, each of which draws about 500 professionals from the industry. The meetings, which are accredited by the state Department of Education, include four half-hour presentations on computer-related topics - two given by customers, one by a vendor, and one by an industry expert.

"It's primarily for the benefit of current customers," says president Warren Rodgers, "but we also identify a number of companies we'd like to be doing business with and invite them as well." The sessions cost the company between $10,000 and $15,000 a year - there is no fee to attend - and Rodgers considers the money well spent. "I think it's the single most important thing we've done in terms of giving our business visibility and credibility in the marketplace. It has set us apart from the competition."

READER'S CHOICE
180

Letter Quality

Don't miss an easy opportunity to **communicate what's important about your business on your company letterhead**.

So says Tom Melohn, of North American Tool & Die Inc. (NATD), in San Leandro, Calif. Across the bottom of NATD's stationery is the statement: "0.1% Customer Rejects Since 1980." This concrete detail about the company's commitment to quality has more impact than an abstract company slogan, he believes.

When customers the company surveyed expressed their incredulity at NATD's low rejection rate, Melohn decided it was just the number that he wanted to keep in front of their eyes.

News That's Fit to Print

Leave it to a public relations firm to teach other businesses how to stretch their own PR dollars. Three years ago Floathe Johnson Associates, a firm in Kirkland, Wash., **began sending news releases on its own progress directly to prospective clients**. Today the releases are the top generator of new business leads for the firm, whose annual sales are $25 million.

About once a month an announcement of a new account, award won, or new hire goes out to 100 members of the press, 150 clients, and 500-plus prospects. One to five prospects call to learn more. Under such circumstances, it can be tempting to turn a news release into a sales pitch. Resist the urge, senior vice-president Chuck Pettis says, or the release will alienate the press and won't impress prospects.

"People say they read about us in the paper," Pettis says. "Nine times out of 10 I bet they are remembering the press release."

Open to the Public

You don't have to be a retailer to build a marketing program around location. Steve Ettridge decided early on to locate offices of his temporary-help service in storefronts, and he believes the decision was a major factor in making Temps & Co. the largest temp firm in Washington, D.C. in just six and a half years. "If image is important to your business," he says, "**it pays to have a storefront**. The best way to project a professional image is to let the public see you."

Four of the company's 12 locations are in retail space, which costs 20% to 50% more than office space. Ettridge also invests in the design and decoration of the reception areas that passersby see. He insists it is well worth the extra cost. "Presenting a professional, upbeat face to the public does wonders for the way people perceive your business." In particular, the store fronts have helped him meet his biggest challenge: recruiting skilled employees to send out on jobs. Ettridge figures that his storefront locations increase the walk-in rate by 50%.

183

"We give our managers
a lot of responsibility, and we expect
them to be fair. A manager
should be able to fire somebody he really
likes and promote a guy who
picks his nose."

GARY HOOVER,
chairman/CEO, Bookstop Inc.

All Present and Accounted for

As a company grows, it can become tough to keep track of who's responsible for what. "You have people constantly crossing functional lines," says Thomas G. Kamp, president of Premier Computer Corp., in Oklahoma City. "It becomes easy for accountability to get lost."

Premier, a disk-drive repair company, has grown from 25 people to about 260 in just four years. "I found myself not knowing who was responsible for ensuring proper turnaround time," Kamp complains. So he **devised a simple system for keeping track of each employee's accountability**, including his own. At least once a year, he asks his 18 executives and managers to draw up a matrix specifying their responsibilities and those of each of the people under them. "By writing it all down, they come to own it," he says.

The matrix looks like this: across the top, employees' initials serve as column headings. Down the side are different job tasks (such as internal growth planning) or limits of authority (such as approving purchases of less than $500). After all the matrixes are complete, Kamp hands them out in a looseleaf binder. "It's a reference tool," he says.

184

The Inside Story

You can't solve problems until you identify their source. If, for instance, you operate a growing retail chain, and you sense that a particular store is underperforming, you're probably going to ask the store's manager what's causing the trouble. Nothing wrong with that, except that you might hear only part of the story. **To find out what's *really* happening**, Richard Schulze suggests you should check in with the checkout personnel - preferably by taking them to breakfast.

"If you've got a problem," advises Schulze, CEO of Minneapolis-based Best Buy Co., a chain of 40 consumer-electronics superstores, "go to the last point the customer visits." In retailing, that means the folks behind the cash registers.

Cashiers hear customer complaints and observe how a store runs, but all too often nobody asks their opinions. After Schulze's most recent cashiers' breakfast, at his Iowa City outlet, he made changes in store-level management.

Schulze says breakfasts work out better than traditional meetings because the relaxed atmosphere helps conversation get started. And the cashiers consider it a nice treat. For $50 to $60, he gets "absolutely invaluable results."

CEO in Training

Putting in a single day on the shop floor to gain employee goodwill may backfire and bring complaints of patronizing behavior. Paul Huber, president and CEO of Seco-Warwick Corp., a manufacturer with 175 employees in Meadville, Pa., was committed to really learning the factory operations, so the floor supervisor assigned him **different jobs for one day a month for a year**.

When he worked as a wire welder, Huber decided the make-do machines were lacking and purchased new ones. Laying brick one day convinced him that using knee pads would be much easier than moving around pads on the floor. And after retracing his steps as an assembly worker, he improved material flow efficiency.

"I gained a much better appreciation of the company's problems," says Huber, who adds that floor employees were impressed with the quick turnaround on improvements. Now the vice-president of manufacturing, Clifford Lohr, has taken over spending one day a month on the floor.

Personalized Wisdom

The problem with new books is that they keep you from rereading the old ones, retailer Stew Leonard says. "You're so busy trying to keep up with what is coming out that you can forget what you've already read. And it's hard to convince yourself to go back and reread a 300-page book."

The owner of Stew Leonard's, in Norwalk, Conn. - an enterprise *Ripley's Believe it or Not!* calls the world's largest dairy store - has come up with a solution.

As he reads useful texts, Leonard underlines passages he likes and scribbles notes in the margins. When he's done, **his secretary types up everything he's marked, and he has a 20- to 30-page new book summary** - which, Leonard says, is better than anything he could buy, because he has personalized it to his business. Periodically he goes back and rereads his summaries.

"You can also give your outlines to employees," Leonard adds. "If you give them a 300-page business book, they'll never read it, because it's too long. But they'll read 30 pages."

187

Use (All) Your Brain(s)

Employees can help solve growth-related problems - provided you give them the opportunity. Last July, Solar Press Inc. shut down its printing plants, rented a nearby community college, and assembled 320 full-time workers for a day of information sharing and brainstorming.

The eight-hour retreat, dubbed Solar Brainstorming day, came complete with T-shirts, catered lunch, and a beer party afterward. Since July is the company's slow month, says company CFO Joe Hudetz, little production time was lost - and the payoff, he thinks, will be substantial. "We know there's no way management can control the company's aggressive growth on their own. We need the help of all the employees to do it."

Top managers gave short speeches, and president and CEO Frank Hudetz presented a slide show on Solar's projected growth and future plans. Employees then met in departmental groups to discuss production bottlenecks, space and equipment needs, staffing requirements, and the like. The upshot: a list of 50 problem areas, each one to be the focus of an employee task force during the coming months.

READER'S CHOICE

188

Value Added

Whenever you go outside to hire a top manager, you run the risk of bringing in someone who doesn't really understand or appreciate your business or your values. William H. Wilson, of Pioneer/Eclipse Corp., in Sparta, N.C., **has a technique for communicating his values to new executives** and giving them an education in the business at the same time. He requires each of them, during the first month of employment, to spend a night working with the company's product.

That would be an inviting assignment if Wilson ran a Porsche dealership, but he makes floor-cleaning systems. So it's over to the high school the executives go for several hours of cleaning, waxing, and polishing the floors, using Pioneer/Eclipse's equipment and products, and often those of competitors as well.

Wilson says that most new executives are happy to do it. "If they think it's beneath them, they're not the kind of people we need."

189

Mixing Business With Pleasure

Entrepreneurs show a remarkable capacity for letting their business screw up their personal lives - remarkable mainly because the solutions are often so simple. Consider Norman Brodsky, the founder of Perfect Courier Ltd. and chief executive of CitiPostal Inc., both located in New York City. While his companies thrived, his family life took a beating, due to his **inability to coordinate his business schedule with his personal commitments**: missing his daughter's recital, forgetting about the school open house, and so on.

Finally, Brodsky and his wife, Elaine, came up with a plan to solve the problem. At the beginning of each month, Elaine now gives him a schedule of family and personal appointments for the next 30 days, which he takes to his office and incorporates into his business calendar. "This way, Norman can decide what he wants to be part of and work his schedule around it," says Elaine. "It saves a lot of headaches."

Says Brodsky, "My life is a lot better balanced than it's ever been."

190

Time Out for Thinking

I f you find you're too busy to do the strategic planning your company needs, you might want to listen to Neal Patterson, chairman and CEO of Kansas City, Mo.-based Cerner Corp. It was when Cerner was doubling revenues about every 45 weeks that Patterson said, "Whoa, I need to preserve some time to think."

He **now schedules a weekly two-hour session to "talk to himself."** He prefers to do it early in the morning - "when my mind is uncluttered" - and away from the office, so he won't be interrupted.

"This isn't fill-in work between appointments," Patterson says, "yet that's how too many executives treat it. That can get a company in trouble."

191

"CEOs who don't use
outside advice run the risk of
internalizing too much.
They never realize their full potential,
and they miss a lot of
opportunities."

GEORGE CLEMENT,
CEO, Clement Communications Inc.

Tailor-Made Expertise

If a board of advisers pays off when planning a company's future, then **why not assemble one when planning for each department**? That's what Lisa Bergson, president and CEO of MEECO Inc., a $4-million maker of scientific measurement devices, figured.

Bergson wanted to revamp the company's outdated image, so she assembled a board of marketing advisers to do a case study of MEECO's marketing efforts. Five outside advisers with years of marketing expertise teamed up with five MEECO people for one long lunch. Bergson left the restaurant with sketches for a new corporate identity, trade booth, and brochure in hand.

"We are in a very technical industry and are located in Warrington, Pa., which is remote geographically. This was one way to keep our people stimulated," says Bergson, who plans to hold marketing and manufacturing advisory meetings next year.

192

Making Time

R ay McCormick, CEO of $30-million American Sweeteners Inc., has weathered three different boards during his company's 15-year history. The experience has taught him a valuable lesson: "**Anyone who is thinking about setting up a board should be prepared to commit at least 10% of his time** to [board-related matters]," he states. "Otherwise, you won't get the right people and you won't get them involved in running your business."

McCormick followed his own advice when he set up his latest advisory council, an informal group of five individuals, first identified through third-party introductions, then interviewed twice by McCormick. Once on board, council members attend four meetings a year at the company's Frazier, Pa., headquarters. Unlike many other CEOs, however, McCormick meets with each member of his council between sessions. It is a responsibility that he feels he shouldn't delegate.

Perhaps the most time-consuming part of this process is deciding what issues should be placed on the council's quarterly agendas, and then compiling background reports on these items for the board. For example, American Sweetener's council recently reviewed the company's strategic planning process, discussed the idea of changing banks, and debated a proposal for a leveraged buyout acquisition.

Do these kinds of responsibilities take away from the time McCormick needs to run his company? The answer is no. "What we're really talking about is running the company," he states. "If you are willing to do the work necessary to set up a good board, you'll wind up with a better company."

193

Wearing Too Many Hats

You may want to **reconsider inviting your lawyer to be on your company's board** of directors. The trouble, says Dennis O'Connor, an attorney with a Waltham, Mass., firm specializing in corporate law, is that things can get confusing when a lawyer is asked to wear two hats - those of business adviser and legal counselor. "There's a gray area in between, and it can be hard for a CEO who acts counter to a lawyer's recommendation to know whether he is risking an illegality or simply disagreeing on business strategy."

An experienced board member himself, O'Connor says it's standard policy at many law firms to sit on the boards of companies they advise, making it difficult for clients to sever the relationships. His own firm has taken a different - and he thinks healthier - approach. O'Connor attends as many as eight board meetings a month, but only as a nonvoting legal and business adviser. Under these well-defined circumstances, in which the voteless attorney wears only a legal hat, having a lawyer attend meetings is a must, O'Connor says.

"Many companies try to save money by not having a lawyer present at all, but that can hold up a decision when a director wheels around and says, 'Let's see what the lawyer has to say about this,' and there's no lawyer there."

194

Locking in Commitment

The high cost of directors' liability insurance, plus the antipathy many chief executive officers feel toward accountability to outsiders, has escalated the formation of informal "advisory boards." Think about it: if you can get the advice without the formal obligation to follow it, are there **any reasons left to have a full-blown board?**

Sandy Brown, president and CEO of Rhode Island Welding Supply Co., thinks there are - as long as you can get around the problem of insurance, which in Brown's case would have cost about $8,000 a year.

Brown says he wanted a board of experienced businesspeople to help him shift his focus from the day-to-day to broader concerns. After months of looking, he found three people who fit the bill and were willing to serve even though the business carries no directors' liability coverage.

Before each quarterly meeting, Brown sends each director an agenda, an update on major developments, and a $250 check. During meetings, Brown expects the directors to challenge him and to point out things he should consider.

But couldn't a bunch of informal advisers do the same thing? Not really, argues Brown. He doubts that the individuals would be as interested or as committed, and he doubts that he himself would be as engaged. "Having a board means I mean business," Brown says.

It also means that he expects his business to endure. If anything ever happened to him, Brown is confident that his directors, with their personal and legal commitments as formal board members, would take charge, and would find a successor to keep the business going.

195

Professorial Advice

If you're like many CEOs, your idea of a good board of directors candidate is the no-nonsense, battle-hardened executive you see yourself one day becoming. That's fine, but to judge by Joe Crugnale's experience, maybe you should **check out ivory-tower intellectuals**, too. An out-of-the-mainstream professor may have a wonderful view of your business's marketplace.

Two years ago Crugnale, CEO of Bertucci's and Bailey's, two small regional restaurant chains, recruited Bert Mendelsohn, a professor of marketing at Boston College who specializes in tracking small food-service chains. "His classes do all my market research and provide me with a lot of information on the competition," says Crugnale. First hired as a consultant, Mendelsohn immediately helped Crugnale with the nuts and bolts: understanding an operating statement, and determining the ratios needed to make his restaurants more competitive.

In short order, Mendelsohn was elected to the board to help plan long-term strategy. For someone like Crugnale, who runs his business primarily by intuition, the mercilessly logical approach of an academic can serve as an effective counterbalance.

Dress Rehearsal Meetings

Mike Allred, CEO and president of Visual Information Technologies Inc., a Dallas graphics-imaging company, wanted to stop employee gossip about his monthly board meetings, so he decided to **hold dry runs of the meetings with his staff** of 90.

"It goes over like gangbusters," says Allred. "Delivering the same spiel we give the board shows we respect employees' participation." Employees ask tough questions, which gears management up for the real McCoy the next day.

READER'S CHOICE

197

MEETINGS

"A group of people working together can come up with smarter decisions than one individual, no matter who he is."

ED HOUCEK,

vice-president, Dewar Information Systems Corp.

Pay the Piper

"The dentist preaches how we must be committed, and then he arrives late to his own meetings," a disgruntled physician's assistant complains. To calm this ubiquitous office gripe, Linda Miles - whose $1.6-million Virginia Beach, Va., company, Linda L. Miles & Associates, gives more than 100 training seminars a year to health-care professionals and their staffs - dreamed up the Tardy Kitty: **for every minute late to a meeting, the culprit must pitch $1 into the kitty.** At quarter's end, the accumulated fines fund a night out for the staff.

Grateful seminar attendees tell Miles that chronic latecomers are now prompt. "The key to its success is that there are no exceptions, because it's usually the leader who is running late," Miles observes.

On-Site Decisionmaking

To cut down on unproductive meetings, Melia Peavey **takes her staff meetings directly to the trouble spot**. "When you're cooped up in a meeting room the problem seems remote," says Peavey, COO of Peavey Electronics Corp., an 1,800-employee electronic musical instrument manufacturer in Meridien, Miss. "By going to the site you get decisions rolling quickly. The different managers can pick up on what needs fixing. The human-resources manager can see how employees work together. The MIS manager sees how employees use the computers. You can stop and question employees on the spot, rather than hearing secondhand what's going on."

When rejects piled up in the raw materials warehouse, for example, Peavey and her managers went right to work by cleaning up the debris and brainstorming about ways to improve operations. Today, the production department sorts rejects by vendor and salvages more parts, purchasing agents make weekly trips to the warehouse to avoid overordering, and the receiving staff takes more care in stacking raw materials.

"Employees are impressed that management is involved and not sitting in offices looking down on everything," says Peavey.

Casual Contact

There's no doubt about it, a growing business can be a professional pressure cooker for employees. To help cool things down at Arche Technologies Inc., Fridays **- when most staff meetings are held - are dress-down days.**

Isaac Levanon, president and CEO of the Fremont, Calif., IBM PC-clone manufacturer, reports the informal environment helps employees loosen up in what could otherwise be a tense meeting. "On Fridays the exchange of information is freer," says Levanon. "People don't say, 'Here's the boss, let's think about what I can say.' It's a nonthreatening environment."

Since instituting the policy, Levanon says, employee morale is up. And every little bit helps when a company grows at a rate of 250% a year to a reported $100 million in annual revenues in 1989.

200

Keep It Brief

Tact and diplomacy may be admirable executive skills, but when it comes to moderating weekly staff meetings, it may be best to dispense with the formalities. Just ask Cecil Ursprung, president of Reflexite Inc., a $20-million reflective-plastic products maker in New Britain, Conn., whose weekly staff meeting recently grew from 6 to 14 people.

"These people have no problem speaking up," says Ursprung. "We realized if everybody contributed at the same rate as when six people attended, it would last half a day." So to keep the contributions brief, he **invested in a $6 alarm clock**. Now, each staffer can stump for six minutes before the alarm rings. "The return on investment is incalculable," quips Ursprung, who says the meetings stick close to the target 84 minutes - and he doesn't have to play the heavy.

READER'S CHOICE

201

Team-Building Projects

It's easy to lose that loving feeling in a fast-growing company. Bryan Beaulieu, CEO of Skyline Displays Inc., a $45-million Burnsville, Minn., maker of portable trade-show exhibits, was looking for a way to unite his 250 employees and 350 independent distributors. "We had drifted apart," he admits.

So, for the **annual sales meeting**, instead of hitting the golf course, Beaulieu organized a project everyone would remember: building a playground. Area residents volunteered time and equipment; employees and the distributors donated engineering and carpentry skills. The cost? Four days of work and $60,000 - the price tag of the usual trek to a golf resort. The event was filmed, and the tape is used for recruiting.

"Whenever we have a bad day," comments Beaulieu, "we go down to the park, watch the kids playing, and get revitalized."

202

Getting Your Money's Worth

I f you're **planning a company retreat**, don't make the common mistake of scheduling meetings from dawn to dusk in a misguided attempt to justify the expense. You'll get just as much accomplished, maybe more, by letting your employees have free time at the beach or on the golf course. "When people get together, they always wind up talking about the things they have in common," says one former *Fortune* 500 executive and veteran sales meeting-goer. "What your people have in common is your company, and that's what they're going to discuss, even if they're playing cards. They'll talk about the accounts they're working on."

Besides, he notes, you're not going to win many points by taking people to a beautiful resort and keeping them cooped up in meetings all day. Better to have focused sessions in the morning and leave the afternoons free. Not only will you have a more successful retreat, but you may get some credit as well.

"Planning is damn scary
if you do it right, because what you're
really talking about is change.
It's much easier to just say,
'Next year's going to be better,'
and leave it at that."

GRAHAM BRIGGS,
VP/finance, Charles River Data Systems Inc.

The Gang's All Here

If you don't have an outside board of directors, you might want to take better advantage of the **advisers you do have - your banker, accountant, and lawyer**. Once a year Pat Bruner, based in Green Bay, Wis., and president of TLC Childcare Centers Inc. and The Chocolate Chicken, gathers her advisers at the bank or in her accountant's office for a day of thrashing out issues of expansion, acquisition, and capital expenditures. "It's a way to explain my vision," says Bruner, "and it keeps me from playing telephone tag and having someone - like the banker - veto my plans later."

The sessions cost about $1,200 in accountant and attorney fees. "I can't stress how cheap that is to get so much worked out," says Bruner, who plans to open two more day-care centers and start a day-care magazine.

204

Plotting Out the Five-Year Plan

How do you keep your employees focused on strategic goals? At Cleveland-based Globe Metallurgical Inc. **managers use a master calendar that shows which team members are working on what**. The calendar keeps the 30 managers at the $100-million-plus producer of metal alloys on track for the year and lets them know who they can go to for help.

On the calendar the blocks for each day contain shorthand references to Globe's five-year plan for improving quality and cutting costs. That plan is a 20-page list of nearly 100 numbered items. So one day's calendar entry might read, "#56 - Curt Goins, visit Union Carbide Corp., perform supplier quality audit." Managers can refer back to the numbered plan for more details and deadlines.

"It's not so much a matter of accountability as what we need to do and when," says Goins, who serves as director of quality at the 250-employee company. "The calendar prods you." Measures like this helped Globe win the Malcolm Baldrige National Quality Award in 1988.

READER'S CHOICE

205

Delegating the Planning

Ask good planners what it takes to make the planning process successful, and you will undoubtedly hear: You **can't plan successfully unless you involve your key managers.**

To many, this may be an obvious point, but to John Sandford, president of a $14-million advertising agency in Memphis, hearing that message during a seminar just about changed his corporate life. Today, Cochran, Sandford, Jones Inc.'s planning committee is made up of company officers and department heads, each of whom has specific areas on which to research and report. Sandford will then tie the reports into a plan that will be presented to the company at large. For Sandford, the process itself has been revelatory. "[This method of planning] is more profitable than the document itself will ever be. Our people are now working together toward the achievement of common goals and shared values."

This same philosophy is shared by 2B System Corp., a plastic-card manufacturing company located outside of Detroit. Instead of the traditional pyramid approach of planning practiced by big companies, CEO James Tyler asks his department heads to do their own operational and budget planning, subject to his final OK. Then, once plans are approved, Tyler says, "I look at my job as being one of a utility infielder. If sales needs help, I'll go there. If production is having problems, I'll shift my weight there."

By asking people to participate in the planning process, says Tyler, you are "putting the challenge on to each individual. It's their goals they are meeting, not yours. It gives them a truer sense of the company's future."

"A lot of people think
that you have to do what we call tit for tat.
That's not so. My theory is
to go up slowly or come down slowly
and then just continue the negotiation.
Keep on talking."

BOB WOOLF,
president, Bob Woolf Associates

Dealing with the Prickly Issues

When two companies merge, there's often a temptation to gloss over tough questions about **which company's culture will be dominant after the merger**. But the failure to resolve such issues can lead to problems down the road.

Last winter, American Star Software Inc. (d/b/a Star Software Systems), in Torrance, Calif., worked out a merger with another software company of about the same size - annual revenues of about $3.7 million. It was to be a merger of equals, with each set of owners holding 50% of the new venture's stock. Neither company would dominate. That, says Star Software president William Webster Jr., was a mistake.

The problem, says Webster, was that the two companies had very different cultures. Star, for example, was a jacket-and-tie outfit, while the other company went for jeans and T-shirts. The other company made loans to employees; Star, which considered its benefits package superior, did not.

"It was very difficult," says Webster, noting that the merger was eventually scrapped for other reasons. "The lesson I learned was that somebody has to be the acquirer. Otherwise, you're asking for trouble."

207

Staying In Until the Final Bell

It's impossible to know too much about a company you're on the verge of acquiring, but lots of CEOs miss a chance to discover more: final negotiations. With all the stress that accumulates, it's a good time to examine the staff you're about to take on. How do they handle pressure? Are they hiding anything?

If you want to find out, Lawrence M. Powers says, push aside the lawyers and **handle the final negotiations yourself**.

Powers is chairman and CEO of Spartech Corp., a Clayton, Mo., plastics manufacturer he has built into a $210-million company with a string of acquisitions - the negotiations for which, he says, have been "very instructive." When the smiling facade across the table breaks down, you learn how people handle conflict. Equally important, you'll be alerted to potential problems within the company if its managers won't yield anything in negotiations.

208

Getting the Full Picture

I f you're looking to buy or sell a company, **how can you screen pro-spective advisers?** Jeff Scheinrock, formerly a senior partner with Arthur Young & Co., who specialized in mergers and acquisitions, suggests asking references for the names of deals that fell through. "If an adviser won't turn them over to you, you're better off looking elsewhere."

Says Scheinrock, who is president of Strolee Inc., a Woodland Hills, Calif., manufacturer of baby products: "Seventy percent of deals fall through. If an adviser doesn't come through with a couple of deals that went sour, or acts as if he's only had successful deals, it's a signal that something's amiss.

"Deals don't go through for a variety of reasons, one of which could be the adviser," says Scheinrock. "You want someone who's secure enough to let you see both sides of their work."

209

Taking Inventory

There's a reason why acquirers **demand three years of audited financials from acquirees**, as William Webster of American Star Software Inc. discovered recently. Eight months ago, he was negotiating to merge his company with another software manufacturer, which was in the midst of its first complete audit. Just to be safe, Webster sent his own team of auditors in to observe. "You'd think that a year of audited financials, checked out by our own accountants, would be enough," he says. "The audit certainly didn't turn up any great cause for concern."

That's because a single audit couldn't catch something like slow-moving inventory. "We later found out that the company had hundreds of thousands of dollars of inventory that simply wasn't sellable, and would have to be written off," says Webster. Fortunately, he discovered the problem in time to cancel the merger. The next time, he says, he'll demand a full three years of audited financials. "If the same dusty boxes show up for three years running, the auditors start to think, 'Maybe it's time to write those things off.'"

210

Point of Reference

Thinking of entering a strategic alliance with a large corporation? Don't feel shy about asking for references - no matter how big the company, advises Mike Allred, CEO and president of Visual Information Technologies Inc., a Dallas-based manufacturer of image processing systems.

Before entering a major strategic alliance with a TRW Inc. subsidiary, Allred asked for contacts at other small companies with which TRW had formed alliances. TRW was happy to comply, and Allred found the information useful. He believes asking for references actually helped him in his negotiating, since it showed he wasn't overanxious to form an alliance. "Winners want to play with winners," Allred observes.

Trust me on this

When companies merge, the "acquired" employees are often uneasy about their new boss and their own job security. The result: lost productivity and low morale. To avoid that pitfall, Bruce Mancinelli, CEO of VM Systems Group Inc., a $10-million software company in Vienna, Va., **conducted welcome interviews to make the new people feel at home**.

On the day VM's acquisition of a division of Systems Center Inc. was announced, Mancinelli met with each of that company's 14 employees. He listened to their concerns and offered them official letters of employment, promising them their current salary, the same or similar job responsibilities, and comparable benefits. Within a week, all accepted.

"It's one thing to buy assets, another to get people involved," he says. "We wanted them to feel like contributors from day one."

READER'S CHOICE
212

SELLING OUT

"It's important to have a plan for
getting out. It keeps you honest.
It forces you to test the value of what you're
doing. When you think about selling,
you have to ask, would anyone else want to be
in this business? If the answer is no,
why are you wasting your time?"

STEVE BOSTIC,
CEO, R. Stevens Corp.

Selling Your Company Short

Everybody likes to feel important, but - when you are selling your company - one of the worst mistakes you can make is to emphasize how essential you are to the business. "If the buyer thinks that the company can't be run without you, it becomes a lot less attractive," says Stan Sanderson, president of Geneva Corp., based in Costa Mesa, Calif.

That may seem obvious, but Sanderson, a man with nine years in the mergers and acquisitions business, says **it is common for owners to undermine their own sales pitches by taking too much credit for a company's successes**, and by exhibiting too much hands-on control. They often do it unconsciously, moreover - stopping in the course of a plant tour, for example, to instruct employees on some detail of their work. A shrewd buyer, says Sanderson, will lower his offer accordingly. Sanderson's advice to sellers: downplay your role (difficult as that may be) and stress the abilities of your management team.

READER'S CHOICE

213

Projecting a Professional Image

If you want to get top dollar when you sell your company, it pays to spend some time and money marketing it to potential buyers. That's what Randall Wise did with his graphics-software business, Graphic Communications Inc. His strategy involved impressing buyers with the company's meticulous organization. Toward that end, he **put out a detailed annual report**, replete with all the goodies found in the annual reports of public companies, including a letter from the president and the chairman, descriptions of products, and financial charts. The project took two weeks of Wise's time and cost $2,500 for 250 copies. "It showed we were trying to run our company professionally," says Wise.

The report had the unexpected effect of improving the company's relations with its banker. Equally impressed was Lotus Development Corp., which bought Graphic Communications in 1986 - and put Wise in charge of analyzing future acquisition candidates.

214

The Ties That Bind

For any chief executive officer who has decided to put his or her business on the block, a crucial issue is **how to retain key managers before and after the sale**. If the most valued employees decide to leave once it becomes clear that a sale is imminent, a CEO has two concerns. In the short term, the value of the company may decrease; in the long term, the exodus of top managers may cripple the ability of the new owners to run the business.

CEOs may want to consider using management contracts and/or a bonus system, but be prepared in some cases, for resistance from buyers who will not want to incur the additional cost. Contracts generally cover one to three years' time and usually include provisions for full salary plus insurance and a pension. Discretionary bonuses can be structured in a variety of ways. For example, a key manager may receive 50% of a cash bonus when the sale is closed, and the remainder 12 and 24 months later. If the company buyer subsequently replaces the manager, the buyer would still pay the amount covered by the earlier agreement, but would not be obliged to pay salary.

One way to defuse problems is to include key management in the negotiations. "Open communication in a sale can go further than monetary rewards to assure that key people remain with the company," notes Orville Mertz, a Milwaukee business broker. Adds Gary Roelke, a senior vice-president in the Teaneck, N.J., office of Geneva Business Services Inc., "In the end, it may be more important for the *buyer* to establish incentives for managers. That goes a long way in forging an important alliance."

215

"Family business - talk about
Greek tragedies revisited.
I swear, the typical founder of a family business
would have no problems whatsoever if he
could be immortal and celibate."

LEON DANCO,
The Center for Family Business

An Insider's Guide to Harmony

When it comes to the delicate matters of family business - like turning a niece or nephew down for a job - typical company rule books don't offer much solace. But J. W. Kisling, CEO of Multiplex Co., a Ballwin, Mo., beverage-dispenser manufacturer with more than 200 employees, rests easy knowing that the **family consensus statement** is on relatives' desks at the office.

The document isn't legally binding, but it does answer commonly asked questions about executive and director qualifications, pay scales, retirement ages, and employment opportunities before they get to Kisling's office. Thanks to the inclusion of some entertaining family history, the consensus statement has enjoyed a friendly reception.

While a few of the 22 family stockholders refused to sign off on the first draft, the objections raised were easily remedied. Has it been used? "To my great surprise, nieces and nephews can cite it. It was definitely worth the trouble," says Kisling.

READER'S CHOICE
216

Pre-Partnership Agreements

You may be hesitant to discuss the **potential breakup of your business partnership** fearing that such talk could prove self-fulfilling. But clarifying sticky questions while your partners are on good terms can help prevent some of the tension that leads to business divorce. And if you *do* decide to split, written agreements can assure that everyone's treated fairly.

"There's an assumption by many partners that even if their businesses fail, they'll be partners forever," says attorney David Gibbs, of Boston's Peabody & Brown. He advises clients to set up an agreement detailing how they'd establish the worth of company stock if one partner wanted out, what each would do if a partner should die, and how to govern the sale of stock to outsiders. For small companies, most such agreements cost between $1,000 and $4,000.

And there's a side benefit, says Gibbs. Partners who can't come to terms on how they'd get out of their relationship might want to rethink getting into one.

217

Paving the Way for Succession

Many company owners would sooner sell the business than set up an outside board, but what about one composed almost entirely of your heirs? At Battery & Tire Warehouse Inc., in St. Paul, Minn., Charles Bodenstab's **board consists of his four children**, aged 25 to 31, as well as his attorney.

The board is actually part of Bodenstab's succession plan. "When I kick off, my kids are the ones who'll inherit the business," he says. The children all live in distant cities, where they pursue their own business careers. One has his own firm; another has a degree from Harvard Business School. By having them on his board, Bodenstab makes sure that they stay informed about the company and have regular contact with employees.

Moreover, the children have no inhibitions about criticizing Bodenstab's plans for the company. "They're very candid," he says. "There's even some competition to see who can be more straightforward." Most important, they force him to deal with tough business problems. "It's awkward to talk about something and then go back and admit you haven't done a damn thing about it." Which may be the best reason for having a board in the first place.

218

A Slow Courtship

If your board of directors is strictly a family affair, you run the risk of a grisly boardroom scene by **nominating a stranger to the board**. To avert such battles, J. W. Kisling, chairman and CEO of Multiplex Inc., a beverage-dispensing equipment manufacturer in St. Louis, went about his boardroom appointments very patiently.

Over a five-year period, Kisling rotated 12 candidates through an informal board of three advisers. This not only gave Kisling a chance to check out the board candidates, but it also gave the three family directors time to warm up to the idea of outside input into their company. Because Kisling had invited the candidates to family social gatherings, the relatives on the board weren't put off when Kisling motioned to vote 3 of the candidates to the board. The family members voted for all 3.

The long-term strategy paid off. Kisling reports the outsiders have provided counsel that's helped Multiplex grow from $10 million to $25 million in seven years. "There are no fights, good exchanges, and very few tie votes," he says.

219

"For small company owners,
there's a "hidden"
management discipline - keeping the
office running smoothly.
When you do it well, nobody notices.
When you mess it up,
all hell breaks loose."

GEORGE GENDRON,
Editor-in-Chief, Inc. *magazine*

Quality Time

Are you getting what you pay for in overtime? Two years ago Jim Read crunched some numbers and confirmed his suspicions: no more was being produced in the 10-hour days that had become standard in his company than had been produced in the bygone era of 8-hour days before The Read Corp.'s business picked up.

"Faces were down, production wasn't up, and there were more accidents," Read concluded after studying the productivity of his Middleboro, Mass., gravel-screening-equipment manufacturing plant. Read was worried, though, that going back to 8-hour days would be hard on his employees, who "had become accustomed to living on the wages of a 55- or 60-hour workweek."

Read now says no to overtime for factory and office employees alike and schedules a second shift instead. But he compensates for the lost pay by issuing three extra paychecks a year, made possible in part by a more efficient factory floor.

Open for Inspection

If your employees don't keep their work areas as tidy as you'd like, take a tip from Max DePree, the chairman of Herman Miller Inc., today a *Fortune* 500 office-furniture maker with sales of more than $700 million. Back in the 1950s, when Herman Miller was a midsize company, DePree discovered a way to keep the building neat that worked better than nagging or giving orders. The secret: holding open houses for families. Herman Miller started the practice to make workers' families feel part of the company, but DePree noticed that the occasions had a nice additional effect. Offices and work spaces would suddenly mysteriously get a good, thorough straightening, as employees prepared for their family guests.

Time-Out

When high quality is the way you get and keep your customers, Scott Hallman reasons, you'd better find a system to maintain it - even if you have to sacrifice growth temporarily. Hallman is CEO of Hospital Correspondence Copiers Inc., a $16-million San Jose, Calif., company that provides medical record-copying services to hospitals nationwide. And key to his sales spiel is the quality of his service - no incorrect records copied, no late delivery. So **when monthly customer checks indicate that quality is dropping, salespeople can take no more new customers** for six to eight weeks.

"Our service is offered on a month-to-month basis," Hallman says, "so customers aren't locked into anything. We have to be vigilantes about quality." The reprieve gives the company the opportunity to hire and train new staff without the added pressure of servicing new clients. And the marketing staff has time to update market analyses, develop new campaigns, and call on prospects without having to close the sale. Does Hallman lose customers? He says maybe 10% of those he turns away look elsewhere. But compared with his chief competitor, he does much better at keeping the accounts he has.

222

No Trespassing

Change can be stressful in a growing business, especially when it trespasses on employees' workspace. Harry Seifert, CEO of $12-million Winter Garden Salad Co., based in New Oxford, Pa., learned the hard way that **morale can suffer if employees aren't updated on revamps that affect their workstations**.

Management redesigned one of the plant's workstations but neglected to tell the employees who use it every day. Suddenly finding their familiar workstation gone one morning bombed with the group. Seifert had thought they'd be thrilled with the new design, but before long companywide morale hit an all-time low. Now, Seifert takes the time to hold quarterly meetings for all 140 employees on such changes. Morale is back up, he reports, and management-employee relations have improved.

Accepting In-House Bids

Next time you sign a hefty check to an outside **janitorial or maintenance service**, think about addressing it to your own employees.

When Harry Brown, president of Erie Bolt Corp., in Erie, Pa., cut his janitorial staff to reduce payroll, he thought of contracting the work out. His employees had a better idea - they wanted to bid on the jobs themselves. Several employees said they would like the added income and would be willing to do the work after hours and on weekends. In fact, they would undercut the outside contractors' prices. Brown decided to give them a shot.

Now, the president of the union does Erie Bolt's snowplowing, and three employees and one company retiree come in regularly to clean the shop and maintain the equipment. They also paint and do minor repairs.

"We're paying less, and there is no doubt that we're getting better service," Brown says. "The employees know the place better, and if they don't do a good job, they know the other employees will get on their case."

Overcoming High-Tech Phobia

We've all heard about computerphobia. More than one company has seen its expensive new high-tech machinery gather dust in a corner because employees can't overcome their reluctance to figure it out. One way to help your people get past the debilitating initial frustration, says Richard Fried, of Kanon Bloch Carre & Co., in Boston, is to have them play games.

Available from stores in wide variety, **computer-game programs can familiarize the fearful with keyboard fundamentals** and elementary commands - while making learning fun. Fried has put games to this use for three or four years now and dismisses the notion that they'll get in the way of real work after they've served their purpose. Most people simply need to learn how to use the keyboard, Fried says. "By playing computer games, people get to know how the cursor moves and how to press those keys quickly. A bond is created between the uninitiated and the computer."

Mail Bonding

Keeping up with the mail can be a colossal task. **To make sure significant correspondence is answered swiftly but carefully**, $6.8-million Measurement Specialties Inc. has a two-step system, says Donald Weiss, CEO of the Fairfield, N.J., manufacturer of measurement devices.

First, within 24 hours a short note goes out to the party saying the letter was received and to expect further correspondence by a specified date - usually within a week. Next, the person in charge of the project that the letter concerns drafts a follow-up letter and lets it sit for a day before sending it around the office for others to read. In the case of proposal writing, the CFO might review the document for overhead expenses, a secretary for grammar, and an engineer for technical specifications.

"Too many companies dash off a reply," says Weiss. "Our customers are prepped for a timely response. And we avoid shooting from the hip."

Planning for Emergencies

At most companies, emergency orders and rush jobs are treated more or less as the stepchildren of the business - work you squeeze in to accommodate a customer in a jam. But Hugh Vestal has discovered that he can satisfy more customers, bring in more business, and manage his company more efficiently by doing the reverse. **Instead of squeezing in the rush orders, he organizes his entire operation around them**.

Vestal's business, Carbide Surface Co., in Fraser, Mich., puts carbide coating on machine tools. When a customer has an emergency, he talks directly with a repairman, who schedules the job. By the time the work arrives, the required machinery is set up and ready to go, thereby reducing the time it takes Carbide Surface to turn the job around. Nonemergency work, meanwhile, is scheduled around the rush jobs, often using machinery that is already set up.

The company used to follow the usual practice of scheduling rush jobs around regular work, says Vestal. "Then it just hit us that this was much easier. And it's been great for business. Often you try to sell a job, and you don't get far until someone says, 'Take this. I need it tomorrow.' When you deliver, the customer has a warm feeling, and the business grows."

227

MANUFACTURING

"Quality is a matter of faith. You set your standards, and you have to stick by them no matter what. That's easy when you've got plenty of product on hand, but it's another thing when the freezer is empty, and you've got a truck at the door waiting for the next shipment to come off the production line. That's when you really earn your reputation for quality."

BEN COHEN,
president, Ben & Jerry's Homemade Inc.

It's Who You Know

If you're looking to subcontract your work to offshore manufacturers, the people in the middle of your trade - the shippers - may be the best source of leads.

Joanne Marlowe, president of DSG Inc., a $4-million Chicago company that sells weighted beach towels, already did business with mills in Brazil and Yugoslavia through U.S. agents. But what she really wanted, she told her shipper, was to **save broker fees by finding offshore mills with which she could work directly**. Her shipper gave her names of contacts at three manufacturers, then made introductory calls on her behalf. She followed up and eventually made the new mills her primary partners.

"When you're dealing overseas, companies are less likely to rip you off if they know you're part of the network," says Marlowe. Bottom line: between cheaper freight and elimination of agent commissions, Marlowe figures she'll save 15% to 17% on costs.

Reducing Lost Work Time

As any factory operator knows, productivity suffers badly when shop-floor accidents cause lost work time. Can simple incentives encourage manufacturing employees to work safer? Melia Peavey thinks so. She **encourages more careful work habits by setting up a daily game of bingo**.

Here's how it works: Meridian, Miss.-based Peavey Electronics Inc. issues bingo cards to employees at each of its manufacturing plants. At the end of any day in which there has been no lost time due to accidents, a number is called over the PA system. Making bingo is worth a $100 U.S. savings bond.

"It works because it's so simple for employees to keep up with," says Peavey, the company's vice-president. "And it makes a nice close to the day."

Since the company introduced the game seven years ago, Peavey reports, the average lost time per employee due to on-the-job accidents has fallen by about 20%.

229

Whistler-Blowers

How do you get employees to care as much about quality as you do? That's a problem Harry Seifert, CEO of Winter Gardens Salad Co., in New Oxford, Pa., thinks he's close to solving. "I'm trying to get employees to throw the rotten potatoes away, not the potato salad," Seifert says, explaining the system he installed in January.

If an employee sees a mistake, such as a bad potato about to go into a salad, he or she sounds the "Matterhorn" - **a horn to blow when something's the matter with the quality of the products**. Everyone gathers around, including the supervisor, and the employee is congratulated for the catch.

The system works, Seifert says, because "employees know we are always looking to improve the system, not to find fault with a person." Horns go off about five times a week, calling attention both to specific slipups, in the hope that they won't be repeated, and to the company's ongoing concern with quality.

READER'S CHOICE

230

Safety Rewards

If you're a growing manufacturer, you're probably fighting a steady increase in your accident and injury rates. Phillip Mayer, president of Luitink Manufacturing Co., a metal stamper in Menomonee Falls, Wis., has a technique that dramatically reduces those costs. Measures such as posters and safety tours, he found, didn't do much good.

Then the company's safety committee hit on the idea of a lottery-style contest. Tickets are given every month to workers with no accidents. Ticket holders are then eligible for a jackpot, awarded every three months, which starts at $250 and is reduced by $50 for every mishap. At the end of the year, depending on the total number of company accidents, employees may be eligible to win two $1,000 prizes (0 to 3 accidents companywide), one $1,000 prize (3 to 5 accidents), one $750 prize (5 to 8 accidents), one $500 prize (8 to 10 accidents), or one $250 prize (up to 12 accidents). No prize is awarded if more than 12 accidents occur. In 1988 there were 4 accidents - compared with 20 in 1987.

If the accident rate stays low for the next two years, Mayer estimates that the company, which posted sales of about $6 million last year, could save as much as $40,000 in insurance premiums. **"We've learned we could not buy safety, but we could buy awareness."**

Driving Home the Point

You can make your manufacturing operation safer by making careful procedures a constant topic for discussion. So says Gordon Lankton, who has transformed the safety performance of his plastic injection-molding factory from substandard to award winning. At every Nypro Inc. meeting - whether held by the board of directors or the warehouse shipping crew - the first topic is always safety.

The issues covered range from how to drive a forklift and stack pallets properly to the development of a boot that won't slip on the clean-room floor. When an accident occurs, it is discussed in detail. Even the annual banquet begins with a year-to-year comparison of time lost due to job-related accidents.

Today the Clinton, Mass., company's annual accident rate hovers between 1 and 2 per 100 employees - which was good enough for an award from the National Safety Council. And healthier employees have contributed to a healthier bottom line. Nypro's workers' compensation bill has been cut from a peak of almost $500,000 per year to just $100,000.

232

"When negotiating prices with suppliers,
I go as far as I can without
hitting their panic buttons. They might lose
money, but they still feel that they've
done a prudent thing."

GARY CINO,
CEO, Step Ahead Investments Inc.

How to Make Friends

Would you like to get better service from your suppliers? You might want to take a tip from Jim Ansara, president of Shawmut Design & Construction Co., in Boston. When he started his business seven years ago, he wanted to differentiate himself from bigger competitors that were pursuing a lot of the same subcontractors and vendors. So he came up with a way to win their loyalty. **Instead of paying the suppliers when he got paid by the customer, as most contractors do, he promised to pay within 30 days**.

Shawmut, with revenues of $40 million, has sometimes had to take out bank loans to make good on its commitment. But as far as Ansara is concerned, the benefits of doing business in this manner far outweigh the costs. The company gets priority treatment from subcontractors - not to mention attractive pricing. "People know they'll be paid quickly," Ansara says, "and that helps position us in the minds of the people we work with. Besides being fair to suppliers, it's been a very good business decision."

READER'S CHOICE

233

Motivating Your Suppliers

It's hard to keep employees motivated, much less a vast network of suppliers. But Harold Plumley, founder of a $70-million industrial-rubber manufacturer, has a solution: **a dose of old-fashioned competition**.

Every May Plumley has invited the top 40 suppliers of Plumley Cos. to a state park in Tennessee for a two-day extravaganza that costs the company $20,000. It features a banquet, golf tournament, magic show, and most important, an awards ceremony. Four prizes are given for outstanding achievement in quality, cost, technology, and market support. "We explain exactly why these suppliers are winners, hoping the others will shoot for those goals next year," says Plumley. His hopes just may have come true. Returns to suppliers have dropped almost 2%, and quality improvements have lowered production waste by another 2%.

234

Getting the Best Prices

If your supplier's sales rep is being unusually cooperative these days, it could be that he's just a terrific guy. Then again, it could mean that you're paying more than you should for your materials. "A supplier's job is to get as much as he can whenever he can get away with it," notes Anne Hallenbeck of A & B Associates Inc., a procurement-consulting firm in Wilmington, Del. Your only real protection is to **line up an alternative supply source**, which can provide you with another perspective on what's happening in your marketplace. Hallenbeck, in fact, advises checking in with the backup at least once a quarter. "That doesn't mean that you need to buy from second sources," she says. On the other hand, you probably can't keep them on the back burner forever, so you should probably figure on sending some business their way sooner or later, or finding some new backup sources.

"Insurance used to be a
relatively simple matter of having a broker
place a policy with an underwriter.
Now it's a matter of finding a policy that
allows you to make a living."

LARRY GOLDBERGER,
president, Garden State Brickface & Stucco Co.

Controlling Insurance Costs

I f you've never checked the way your business is classified for insurance risk, maybe you should. As Craig Hickerson discovered, an unchecked mistake can be costly.

Hickerson's lesson came in the form of a bill for workers' compensation coverage at a new branch office of his company, Kansas City, Mo.-based Hickerson Cable Installation Inc. Instead of the $1.80/$100 rate he was used to paying, the price had jumped to more than $3/$100. The reason? Hickerson had been classified with the kind of companies that string cable lines between telephone wires, something it doesn't do. Many of the company's installations, in fact, are *underground*. "The insurance salesman thought he could slip it by me," Hickerson says. "I gave him the code we're normally classified under, and he was pretty surprised."

There are some 400 workers' compensation classifications, with rates from as little as 48¢/$100 for clerical businesses to more than $60/$100 for bridge workers. General-liability classifications are even more numerous - there are 700 to 800 of them. And liability classification errors are much more common than those for workers' comp. Call your agent today.

236

Keeping the Injured Involved

Do you write off injured workers - approve the workers' compensation claims, shuffle in replacements, and forget the wounded until their months on the dole are over? If so, you may be missing an opportunity.

Employees who are injured on the job don't necessarily have to be lost to workers' comp, says Thomas Lynch, of Lynch, Ryan & Associates Inc., a benefits consulting firm in Westboro, Mass. Companies can bring many of the injured back to do light tasks around the factory or office, thereby raising productivity, lowering insurance costs, and boosting morale at the same time.

"Think about tasks you've always wanted done but never had people around to do," Lynch says. "Weed through them: some can be done seated, others with one hand." Then, says Lynch, negotiate a temporary job description together with the injured employee and his or her doctor. In cases in which light or restricted work is possible, Lynch claims that many employees will accept the offer.

In addition to getting worthwhile tasks accomplished, companies that routinely issue this policy - and have at least 80 to 100 employees insured under what is known as a loss-sensitive plan - can receive refunds of 40% or more on their annual workers' compensation premiums, according to Lynch. Smaller companies usually don't qualify for refunds, but they may eventually get lower premiums.

READER'S CHOICE

237

Read the Fine Print

Think twice before signing up for one of those "claims-made" **liability policies** that insurance companies offer. These are the policies that provide coverage only for claims made during the time the policy is in effect. In contrast, a traditional "occurrence" policy protects you even if the claim is made years after the policy has been terminated.

Claims-made policies have one major selling point: they start out cheaper than occurrence policies. Eventually, the premiums rise to comparable levels, but by then you're locked in. That's where the danger lies. If, at that point, you decide to switch to an occurrence policy or other insurance alternative, you won't be covered for claims dating back to the claims-made period - unless, that is, you have a "tail" policy, which may cost up to 200% of your annual premium.

"To an accountant,
saying you don't have a general ledger
is like saying there is no such
thing as God."

CHUCK SUSSMAN,
president, Pretty Neat Industries Inc.

Less Filling, Sells Great

When a large corporate customer tries to throw its weight around on a purchase, ordering, say, 10 truckloads of goods with 120-day terms, it can send a small company's budgets and cash flow into chaos. Jim Anthony, CEO of Delta Technology International, a software company in Eau Claire, Wis., **talks his customers into buying less - at least for the short term**.

When Delta's salespeople make a call on a prospective customer, they recommend that a buyer test five or six copies of its software to get acquainted with the program and then equip one department at a time. By selling amounts that the large company's buyer can personally sign off on, Delta avoids the problems of receiving unsigned purchase orders or having to wait for decisions to be made at committee meetings, which can drag out and even kill deals.

Seven-year-old Delta's $99 menu-system software program, called Direct Access, ranked in the top 20 of corporate titles on a 1989 industry best-seller list, so the strategy appears to work. "And without the accompanying headaches," says Anthony.

239

Auditing Your Auditor

Beware the auditor who insists that you keep your chart of accounts in tax-return sequence or in alphabetical order with no numerical codes. In effect, he is having you maintain your books for his own convenience in preparing his report and your tax returns. Aside from those documents, you are not likely to get anything of value from the relationship - certainly not insight into the finances of your company. As a result, you may wind up making serious, and avoidable, mistakes due to a lack of reliable information.

The solution is to **find an auditor who will help you set up sound financial reporting systems, with information updated on at least a monthly basis**. If you have a bookkeeper handling your finances, you should insist that the auditor help train that person to monitor the key variables in your business. "In the long run, the best answer is to develop your own in-house financial expertise," says Robert Kelly, president of C.E.O. Consulting Services Inc., in Peabody, Mass., and a CPA.

Teaching the Bottom Line

You probably won't improve a losing operation unless you can **get your managers, especially ones who don't usually think in bottom-line terms, to understand the financial consequences of every decision they make**. And Ken Hendricks, CEO of American Builders & Contractors Supply Co., has found a dramatic way to do just that. He educates his people with Monopoly money.

Hendricks routinely acquires wholesale outlets operating in the red and tries to turn them around. To help his managers understand where the money's going, he sets up two shoe boxes, one representing the center's budget, the other its expenditures. As the managers move play money into the budget box, they see the consequences of plans gone awry - poor maintenance, for example, or overstaffing. The consequences are personal, too; the managers' compensation is determined by the center's performance.

"When a tire blows on one of our trucks, it costs you in profitability and profit sharing," says Hendricks. "It hits the managers like a ton of bricks. This gets people to see reality."

READER'S CHOICE
241

Surviving a Cash Crunch

Sometimes it pays to keep your problems to yourself. That's what Jim Ansara decided when he suddenly discovered in late 1985 that his company, Shawmut Design & Construction, was $550,000 in the hole due to poor financial controls. While he worked to solve the problems, he kept vendors and subcontractors in the dark by paying bills in 30 to 35 days, much faster than the industry average.

The trick, of course, was coming up with the cash. To do that, he took only high-margin jobs for customers he knew would pay promptly. When possible, he completed work ahead of schedule and billed some jobs twice a month. He also convinced a few customers to pay for work up front, in exchange for a discount.

The plan worked so well that suppliers never suspected the company was in trouble. As a result, Ansara had the time he needed to get the company back in the black.

"You can't cut costs
when you're sitting there driving your
leased Mercedes from your palatial home.
You've got to come
back down to reality and become
part of the troops."

DAVID FERRARI,
president, Argus Management Corp.

The Price Is Right

Cost-cutting isn't fun no matter how you do it, but a little gamesmanship can help. When Sundance Spas, a Chino, Calif., plastic hot-tub-maker, **launched a one-year program to reduce its cost of goods sold, it began with a rousing, companywide session of "The Price is Right."**

"It taught purchasing agents in a few minutes why it's important to tell people the value of things," says CEO Ron Clark. In one instance, employees guessed that a plastic part frequently broken during manufacture cost only $2, and then discovered that its actual price was $32.40. "Just six weeks after they learned that, the production people came up with a two-piece design for the part. Now, when the piece has to be replaced, it costs us $2 rather than $32.40."

Almost across the board, Sundance employees were surprised by how much they'd underestimated costs, and many of them offered suggestions for savings. Says Clark: "If you've got to do some belt-tightening, I think the game is a lot more effective way to break the news than handing out a memo informing supervisors their budgets have been cut."

243

Just Say No (to High-Cost Drugs)

You're not the only one who's eager to battle the rising cost of medical insurance. After watching his company's premiums increase by more than $500,000 over five years, Jack Stack of Springfield Remanufacturing Center Corp. (SRC) gambled on a way to slow the tide: SRC **now self-insures the prescription-drug portion of its insurance plan**.

Under the previous program, employees filled prescriptions without ever seeing a bill. Since there was no incentive to limit costs, price was never an object - and the big spending resulted in premiums that were about to run SRC $70,000 a year. Well, Stack decided, why don't we pay for the prescriptions ourselves, arrange for volume discounts, and give employees a reason to think twice about costs?

It worked. SRC canceled its prescription-drug insurance, struck off-price deals with area pharmacies in grocery chains, and offered a special bargain-rate deductible on purchases of generic drugs. Encouraging the use of generics - something insurance companies don't do - can reduce the prescription-drug outlay of the company's 425 employees and their families by more than 40%.

How has the change affected the program as a whole? What would have been a $5,000-per-month insurance bill is now a $1,800-per-month pharmacy bill. That will add up to almost $40,000 in savings for SRC in one year.

244

Give and Ye Shall Receive

If you don't own a piece of the company, you tend not to lose much sleep over runaway costs - which is a problem for those who *do* own the company. But Philip Edelstein has **found a way to make his employees care about cost control, and he's done it without giving up equity in his business**, Danbury Plumbing Supply Co., in Danbury, Conn.

Every month, Edelstein posts a chart of the company's gross sales and expenses. He also puts 15% of profits into a "mini-bonus" pool. The bonuses are then distributed each month to all 20 employees, using a formula that takes into account their salary level and seniority. Edelstein says that, "about five minutes after I started it," employees began turning out lights and closing doors. The company's warehouse is now warmed by two big heaters, instead of seven. "It can be 45 degrees in there, but they don't mind," he says, "because they know it will come back to them."

Last year, Edelstein handed out about $100,000 in mini-bonuses. Meanwhile, employee productivity has soared. Danbury's sales per employee are about $400,000, twice the industry average.

READER'S CHOICE

245

You May Be Entitled to a Refund

Thinking of exporting a product with some imported components? Be sure to ask your customs broker about the U.S. Customs Service's duty-drawback program. **Under duty drawback, an exporter can get a refund for 99% of the duty paid on the imported item** - even if someone else did the importing.

Example: Carstab Products, a $55-million chemical company in Reading, Ohio, imports an acid from Germany that it uses in making plastic products. Carstab then exports $12 million of its finished products all over the world - and gets back all but 1% of the duties paid on the acid in the exports. That refund amounted to about $50,000 in one year.

"Duty drawback has been around since 1789," says Harold Lemesh, chief of the liquidation branch of the San Francisco Customs District. "But there are still probably hundreds or even thousands of companies that have never heard of it."

Negotiating Accounting Fees

You may have more leverage than you think when it comes to hiring an accountant. The major accounting firms are so anxious to build their growth-company clientele these days that **you could be in a good position to negotiate favorable rates**.

"It's generally possible to get one of the 20 largest firms to give you a fixed rate for three years," notes Judson Beamsley, president of Tek-Aid Industries Inc., a distributor of microcomputer products in Arlington Heights, Ill. "We dropped the fee for a full audit from $27,000 to $17,000 under a three-year contract guarantee."

Of course, you may have problems keeping your rate down when the contract ends. Beamsley, for one, was notified that his national accounting firm planned to raise its fees by 50% at the expiration of its contract. "So we contacted another large firm and negotiated a rate that was $2,500 less per year than the previous fee," he says gleefully. "It's like anything else - the fee is always negotiable, and people who don't negotiate pay."

247

Charming the Cobra

The federal law known as COBRA (Consolidated Omnibus Budget Reconciliation Act) may contain a hidden bonus for some small companies - a provision that will allow many of them to **save money on the benefits they offer employees hired away from larger companies**. The provision requires employers to give departing employees the option of continuing their health-insurance coverage for up to 18 months. The employee has to pay for the coverage, but the tab can't be more than 2% over the employer's cost. Since large companies enjoy a significant rate advantage (often 20%, by one estimate), a small company may find that it makes sense to reimburse new employees for continued coverage under their previous plans.

The reimbursements would, of course, be taxable income for the employee, which could reduce, or even eliminate, the savings to new employers who cover the tax as well as the insurance cost. But COBRA could prove a boon to other companies, especially start-ups, notes William J. Cammock, president of Cammock, Cammock & Tallitsch Inc., a benefits-and-compensation consulting firm in Cleveland. Some of them may find that the law lets them avoid the hassle of establishing health-insurance plans altogether, at least during their early months of operation.

248

Controlling Sky-Rocketing Travel Costs

Airfares and hotel charges change so frequently it sometimes pays to have a person on staff whose job it is to be your **in-house travel agent scouting out the bargains**. While working with an outside travel agency to make the actual travel arrangements, this person could be examining the company's overall travel requirements and suggesting bulk deals or employee policies to save costs.

Some ideas might be:

*Restricting your traveling employees' use of their frequent-flyer miles to business travel - but paying them a portion of the savings.

*Double checking to see that hotels aren't sending room charges to both the company and the traveler's personal account.

*Negotiating bulk discounts from airlines, hotels, and other vendors.

*Since many domestic airlines offer fares that are about 50% less if you stay over a Saturday night, encouraging traveling employees to do so by picking up the weekend hotel bill - or sharing the savings in fares.

*For employees traveling toward the end of the week, comparing daily rental car rates with weekend rates, most of which run Thursday through Sunday.

249

White-Collar Rescue

Sometimes it is managers - not the rank and file - who need to be saved from the budget ax. Combustion Engineering Inc., a diversified manufacturer in the oil, gas, and power industries, headquartered in Stamford, Conn., decided to cut labor costs at one of its plants when there was a temporary drop in work load. The blue-collar work force was unionized, and contracts stipulated that layoffs be made on the basis of seniority. Therefore, the company divided the supervisors into four groups of roughly 10 people each, and rotated them in week-long layoffs for four months. The rotating layoffs helped the plant, located in East Monongahela, Pa., **survive the slowdown without having to resort to permanent layoffs**.

"The layoffs spread the burden and saved people's jobs," says company spokesperson Kevin Pilon. "If we had to, we'd do it again."

250

Cutting the Cost of Customized Software

Six years ago, Paric Corp., a $40-million construction company in St. Louis, realized it could no longer rely on prepackaged software to meet its specialized demands. At the same time, it knew that for many companies its size, the cost of customized software could be staggering.

Paul McKee, Paric's chief executive officer, came up with an interesting strategy. He enlisted the aid of contract programmers over a five-year period to set up, and continually refine, a customized software package for such functions as subcontractor bidding and accounting. Last year, when the finished product began to generate interest from local construction companies, Paric set up a new division - Paric Computer Solutions - to sell and market the program.

"We **had spent so much time and money developing our software, we figured we could offset some of those costs by actually selling it to other companies**," says McKee. He expects Paric Computer Solutions, staffed by two salespeople and five programmers, to sell more than $500,000 worth of software in its first full year.

251

Turning Garbage into Gold

You may be throwing away money with your garbage, especially if it includes a large volume of recyclable products. That's what George Mellios discovered when he became vice-president of logistics for Vienna, Va.-based Entre Computer Centers, a franchisor of computer retail stores. Appalled that the company was spending more than $70,000 a year to haul away corrugated packing material, Mellios contacted a local paper recycler, who agreed to buy it. The proceeds (about $275 per month) cover the rent on a bailer, which Entre uses to flatten the boxes. Meanwhile, the company has cut its trash-removal costs by more than 85%, or about $5,000 per month - the equivalent of one fairly well-paid executive.

Of course, few companies are as trash-intensive as Entre, but Mellios estimates that recycling can benefit even those spending as little as $5,000 per year on trash removal. And you can probably save more if your local recycler doesn't require bailing, or if you happen to be near a large company that already uses a recycler.

"We don't want to ruin
a business relationship by having a haphazard,
obnoxious bill collector.
Keeping up on late payers is
like shaving — if you don't do it every day
you look like a bum."

WILLIAM DONOHOO,
The Gibson Group Inc.

Flexible Payments

Sometimes you're better off asking customers when they want to pay their bills, instead of assuming that they will all pay net 30 days. Burjon Steel Service Inc., in Springboro, Ohio, tried that approach and found that it gained leverage with customers at no additional cost.

Before closing a sale, Burjon makes a point of finding out exactly what terms of payment it can expect from the customer. If the customer wants to pay in, say, 60 days - and that seems reasonable - Burjon then **builds the expense into its price estimate, taking into account its own borrowing costs**. Down the road, Burjon will often encourage the customer to pay on a more timely basis, offering a half-percent discount for payments received in 45 days, 1% for those received in 30.

Unconventional as Burjon's flexible payment policy may be, it has helped the company build strong relationships with customers - and has also given Burjon an edge on its competitors, which tend to be conservative in such matters.

253

Red Alert

At Decoma Industries, staying on top of accounts receivable is everybody's job, including the president's. On the Vernon, Calif., architectural firm's **project-scheduling board, a red dot goes up next to the names of late-paying customers. Employees halt work on those clients' projects.** "It keeps us focused on profitable projects rather than on the ones for which we have the most emotional investment," says president Steve Notaro.

The red dot goes up if an invoice payment is one day past due (30 days after it's mailed). Notaro mails or faxes the customer a copy of the invoice with a note saying work has stopped. He follows up with a letter every 15 days. Each day he personally calls the two most delinquent customers. Notaro has used the approach since the company's founding, 12 years ago. Decoma, a $2.5-million business, has never had a bad debt.

Goal-Oriented Collections

Passive approaches cripple most companies' accounts-receivable systems, according to Ron Schneider, controller of Motif Designs Inc., a $10-million wallpaper and fabric manufacturer in New Rochelle, N.Y. "Most companies let their clients determine their cash flow, instead of proactively managing their accounts receivable."

At Motif Designs, Schneider **sets weekly collection goals for his staff based on his assessment of the company's cash-flow needs**. Even more unusual, he leaves it up to his employees to decide which accounts are most profitable for them to focus their attention on. Schneider reinforces his system with a biweekly bonus that rewards each individual according to his or her own performance, based on mutually agreed-on goals. Results have been impressive. Due in large part to the increased cash flow from accounts receivable, Motif has been able to reduce its bank borrowings by 20%.

255

Cutting Your Losses

Reading bankruptcy announcements may not be your idea of fun, but it could help save your company money if one of your customers goes belly up. Under the law, **you have the right to reclaim any items shipped to a newly bankrupt company, provided you give the customer or the bankruptcy court notice within 10 days of delivering the goods**. The one restriction: you may lose the right to reclaim the delivered goods if they have been used as collateral for an obligation of the bankrupt company.

Since you have to act fast to invoke your reclamation rights, it helps to have an early warning that a customer is in trouble: keep a close watch on questionable accounts. As soon as you learn of a bankruptcy, moreover, make your claim right away. "If the company is in a different city, ask a business associate there to write the letter for you and deliver it himself," advises Boston bankruptcy attorney Daniel C. Cohn. "Make sure that the letter identifies the items and gives formal notice that you're reclaiming them."

Offering an Incentive to Pay

S oil Shield International **has cleaned up its collections by stuffing a discount coupon in with invoices**. If customers pay the invoice within 15 days, they'll get 5% off the next purchase of the company's fabric protector. "If a furniture retailer normally buys $1,500 worth, he sees a coupon worth $75 and says, Wow," says Mike Connolly, president of the $13-million-a-year company based in Fremont, Calif. "Because it looks like cash, it's more attractive than an offer in a letter."

In the four months after the first coupons were offered, the program helped slash average outstanding accounts receivable from 50 to 40 days. What's more, the coupon has encouraged future sales.

257

Hiring the Big Guns

When a credit manager trying to collect on delinquent accounts has struck out more often than the Cleveland Indians, it may be time to call in a commercial collection agency. **Collection agencies, especially during economic downturns, can be an effective way to speed up receivables**, provided a company is careful about which agency they use.

Those that are willing to make personal visits to delinquent customers should be high on the list of candidates. "We don't want someone who can write letters and telephone," says Evelyn Hesketh, credit manager at H. W. Baker Linen Co., in Mahwah, N.J. "We've already been doing that right along, with no success. You need someone who knows the law and has the experience to deal with tough clients." Most agencies charge clients on a contingency basis, averaging about 25% of the amount collected.

Also, credit managers should look for agencies that belong to the Commercial Collection Agency Section of the Commercial Law League of America, which establishes guidelines concerning operations and ethics, and requires bonding of all members.

From the agency's point of view, timing is important in its relationship with clients. "We're not miracle workers," says Russell Farnham, a consultant with the agency of Bruhnke & Silver, headquartered in New York City. "If an account is six to nine months past due, there is a real deterioration in the probability of collecting. We like customers to call us earlier rather than later, somewhere from 90 to 120 days past due."

No Pay, No Work

James Stroop, president and CEO of $12-million Lakewood Inc., a construction company in Holland, Mich., takes a hard line when it comes to getting paid. **He stops work on any job for which payments are 20 days overdue**.

"We bill for projects monthly, sending out invoices on the 25th of the month," Stroop explains. "Payment is due on the 5th or 10th day of the following month. By the 12th day, I get a list of customers whose payment hasn't been received." On days 15 through 18, Stroop and his account managers hit the phones, warning delinquent payers that projects will be shut down if payment isn't received promptly. "Usually we don't have to take further action," he notes. But if customers don't pay up, construction grinds to a halt on day 25, only to be resumed after a cashier's check is deposited in Lakewood's coffers.

Lakewood has written off less than $5,000 worth of bad debt in the company's 15-year history. "If you're dealing with regular customers, they won't want to see their shipments or services interrupted," reasons Stroop. "Companies have lots of leverage - all they have to do is be willing to use it."

READER'S CHOICE 259

Closing the Sale (Completely)

Any company that says it has never had an accounts-receivable problem either isn't looking very hard or isn't selling very hard. Meanwhile, those thousands of companies that do suffer from bad debt might consider a strategy that Macke Business Products Inc., in Buffalo and Rochester, N.Y., has been using for 15 years: **tying salespeople's commissions to the collection of receivables**.

At Macke, a $13-million office furniture and supply company, a salesperson's commission is reduced by 5% if an account is 60 days past due; at 90 days past due, it is reduced by 10%; at 120 days, the commission is lost altogether. "It depends on how you define a sale," says Larry Romano, head of the company's Buffalo office. "It's not just a matter of going out and getting [it], but also of getting paid."

The theory behind Macke's approach is that a call to a delinquent customer from the company's credit department is probably less effective, and more alienating, than a reminder from the salesperson in charge of the account. As for the sales force itself, the system encourages greater awareness of customers' financial stability. Salespeople go on every sales call with a binder that includes not just a weekly sales printout and an inventory sheet, but also a monthly aging report on that particular account's payment history.

Preventing Discounting Abuse

Having trouble with customers who take their early-payment discount even when they don't pay early? Carl Hansen, president and CEO of Viking Engineering Inc., a Tarpon Springs, Fla., manufacturer, has a solution.

Instead of detailing the discount on an invoice, making it tempting to take the discount regardless of when paid, Hansen prints his early-payment price offer only on an eye-catching green coupon included with each bill. The separate coupon prevents payables clerks from honestly confusing the discounted price with the regular, net-30 billing. It also, says Hansen, "psychologically grabs the customer and bumps us up the list of people to be paid."

Apparently, it works: Viking's average bill is paid in a respectable 35 days - down from 55.

A Check in Hand

If a customer wants you to ship a product (or provide services) but you aren't sure of his credit, he or she may suggest giving you a post-dated check. Don't think that this solves your problem. After all, the customer could always stop payment, or the check might bounce.

On the other hand, **a post-dated check is probably a little better than a verbal promise**, which may be the only alternative. If you decide to take the check, however, be sure to consult a lawyer. Some states require that you remind the customer you have it, and are planning to cash it, a few days prior to the date it comes due.

262

Protecting Against Fraud and Theft

Richard Rampell, a CPA in West Palm Beach, Fla., warns that many companies have only the loosest of procedures to handle bad-debt write-offs, which leaves them exposed to collusion between the members of their accounting staffs and delinquent customers. "Companies **should set up formal mechanisms to control the points at which debts are either turned over to attorneys or collection agencies or written off** - none of which should be able to happen without the signed approval of the company's CEO or CFO," Rampell advises. He also recommends setting up an accounts-receivable control total to make sure that all changes have been credited properly and that they match. The total deposits on sales should agree with the total payments of the individual customers as they have been recorded on each of their accounts-receivable balances. These should be compared with the accounts-receivable control total monthly. It's a way to make sure that there have been neither careless mistakes nor thefts.

"All the entrepreneurs
I know want to retire and become
venture capitalists. But all the
venture capitalists I know want to retire
and become entrepreneurs."

STEVAN BIRNBAUM,
Oxford Partners

Character Loans

For start-ups, it's a classic catch-22 situation. You can't get a loan without a track record, and you can't get a track record without a loan. Richard Aman, CEO of ProKnit Corp., in Scottsdale, Ariz., found a way out. He **built his credit record before building his business**.

Although ProKnit wasn't incorporated until 1984, Aman began filling out personal-loan applications in 1980. His first loan was for $4,000 or $5,000, unsecured and payable in 90 days. "I said to my banker, 'When I come back and ask for a big loan to start my business, I expect you to be there for me,' and he was," Aman says. Over the next five years Aman paid off more than 10 loans, escalating the stakes to a $100,000 one-year unsecured note, needed to fill his first big order when he started ProKnit. The apparel-manufacturing business has grown from $331,000 in sales in 1985 to more than $14 million in 1988.

Where Money-Finders Fail

A first-time search for venture capital can be awfully confusing. Some entrepreneurs, unfamiliar with the jargon and uncertain about which steps to take and when, turn to money-finders - people who help write business plans and peddle them to venture firms. Trouble is, **with many venture firms the presence of a money-finder can jeopardize your chance of making a deal**.

"Money-finders are a distraction," says C. Richard Kramlich, of New Enterprise Associates, in California. "We're not bidding on the money-finder, we're bidding on the people who want to start a business. When I see finders, it's a negative."

Other venture financiers echo Kramlich. All agree that general networking within the finance community is a better way to connect with venture sources. They note that the best tips leading them to new companies often come from bankers or lawyers whose recommendations aren't made for a price. Still intent on hiring someone's help? Then at least be sure you never pay a fee up front, say the venture folks. Pay *only* upon completion of a deal.

Raising Money Without Giving Up Control

What most founders fear when it's time to raise money is losing control. The fear isn't groundless. Many entrepreneurs who sell a majority of their stock in order to bring in capital are later thrown out by investors when times get tough. Robert Ronstadt, CEO of Lord Publishing Inc., has a solution.

When Ronstadt became a minority shareholder in his Natick, Mass., software publishing company last year, he **retained operational control by establishing a voting trust**. He now owns 43% of Lord Publishing's stock, but controls 79% of its voting shares. Because the five trustees include Ronstadt, his wife, and another relative, he can heavily influence the entire bloc of its shares.

Ronstadt set up the trust for 20 years. But the important thing, he says, is that entrepreneurs protect their positions at least until their companies reach a period of stability, which he defines as 12 months of positive operational cash flow.

Ronstadt concedes that investors may demand more shares or a lower share price in return for giving up their voting rights. He argues that a voting trust is well worth this cost. "It's imperative that the lead entrepreneur maintains the management control to fulfill his vision for the company," he says. "The opportunity for Monday-morning quarterbacking is incredible."

266

Finding the Smart Money

I f you need capital to expand your business, don't assume that an investment banker has the answer. "Investment bankers want you to think that they own the capital markets," says Daniel Kolber, president of Kolber Securities Corp., in Atlanta, who raised $90 million as executive vice-president at Air Atlanta. "But if you're resourceful and willing to do the legwork, you don't need them," at least not when you're looking for modest sums of, say $50,000 to $2 million.

Kolber - who has raised capital for everything from oil-and-gas partnerships to real estate deals to start-ups - says **public records of real estate purchases and other investments can prove invaluable for leads**. For one thing, they'll identify people who have "the assets and the inclination." Where can you find the appropriate records? That depends upon where you live. In most states, real estate records are kept at the local registry of deeds. For the names and addresses of limited partners, you may have to visit the secretary of state's office or a county recorder's office. If you're looking for investors in a public partnership, you generally have to check the back pages of prospectuses.

Once you've lined up your investors, all you need is a good lawyer to structure the deal.

The Friendliest Investors of All

Charles Bodenstab likes to keep his revolving credit line at his bank as open as possible in case he needs it. So to meet his short-term cash requirements, Bodenstab, president of Battery & Tire Warehouse, in St. Paul, Minn., **taps into a source closer to home: his children, friends and employees**. Lately, he has borrowed about $100,000 in this manner. The "commercial paper" is offered in $10,000 bites, and each month investors receive interest checks for 1% of their $10,000 investment.

Bodenstab says he's happy to pay his investors, who include three of his four children, an annual amount of $1,200. "That's about what my incremental borrowing cost is. And it keeps me from having to pay late fees to my vendors," he says. He gives investors letters acknowledging their investment. And if they need the money? "All they have to do is let me know. We pay them instantly."

268

Picking Your Investors

Contrary to popular opinion, you don't have to abandon your fate to anonymous investors when you take your company public. Just ask Michael E. Cope, founder and CEO of Interphase Corp., in Dallas, who **has managed to keep pretty good control of his company's destiny by seeking out the kind of investors he wants**.

Cope developed his strategy prior to Interphase's initial public offering in early 1984, as he traveled around the country making presentations to prospective investors. Instead of leaving the follow-up to the underwriters, he and his top managers kept track of the participants who asked the best questions, and then met with them afterwards. "We tried to avoid investors whose natural tendency would be to dump the stock when things got rough," says Cope.

So far, the strategy has worked. The company raised $4.5 million from its 600,000-share offering, which it sold to about 350 investors. Most of the big ones held onto their stock during a bad stretch a few years ago. Cope, for his part, has kept them well informed about the business. "With a public firm, you won't have total control," he says. "But if you play your cards right, you can have a lot more than you'd expect."

Keeping the VC Door Ajar

One of the hardest things about raising money from venture capitalists is getting in to see them. Business plans arrive on their doorsteps hourly, and when the market for new issues is deader than John Travolta's career, they're not all that eager for deals.

"You can't call them daily -they don't want to deal with a pest. Yet you want to stay on their agendas," says Michael M. Nightingale, president and CEO of GMIS Inc., in Malvern, Pa., who has discovered a way to do just that.

Nightingale, whose company makes software for the health-care industry, keeps a file of every venture capitalist who has ever expressed even the vaguest interest in GMIS. "Whenever there's new information, we do a mailing," he says. Sending the letters makes it easier to get his calls returned, he says. It must be working: so far the company has raised more than $6 million.

270

"We're not like venture capitalists.
We're like Hertz Rent-a-Car. When they rent
you a car, they charge you for usage,
and they expect to get the car back.
When we give you a loan, we charge interest,
and expect to get our money back."

ROGER V. SMITH,
president/CEO, Silicon Valley Bank

Playing Hard to Get

The rule with most bankers is that they are glad to lend you money when you don't need it, and reluctant when you do. That psychology can spell problems for companies, but at least one chief executive officer we know has used it to maintain a healthy line of credit for the past four years.

"My advice is, **get approval for more than you need, then don't use it**," says Jud Beamsley, president of Tek-Aid Industries Inc., based in Arlington Heights, Ill. He currently has a $3.5-million open line of credit, of which he has never used more than $2.5 million. Indeed, he generally spends less then 75% of any loan. "If you never take the last dollar, they're always asking you to borrow more."

Nor does Beamsley hold on to the money, as many companies do. Instead, he sharply reduces his loans once or twice a year, which - he says - makes his banker wonder if he's leaving. He also makes a point of leaving another lender's loan proposal and business card on his desk whenever his own banker comes to visit. It's a psychological game, he admits, but it works.

271

Going Once, Going Twice ...

By 1986, after 16 years in business, Susan Bowen, CEO of Champion Awards Inc., a $7-million screen printer in Memphis, was tired of dickering with bankers. Her solution was to **treat banking business like any major business purchase: put it out to bid**. Bowen sent a package to four banks detailing her business's financial history, outlook, and banking needs. She closed her cover letter with "The best bid wins."

The result? A more generous line of credit, better interest rates on long-term loans, and a surge in her banker's competitive spirit. When her banking package went out for bids in 1988, her current bank kept her business by meeting another banker's lower bid.

272

Prove Your Banker Wrong

Suppose you've shopped your borrowing needs and decided that the lender you *really* want to work with is too pricey. You negotiate hard for an upfront rate cut, but the bank won't budge. **Is there anything else you can do to persuade your banker to reduce your interest expense?**

Probably, says Dean Treptow, CEO of First Bank Brown Deer, in Brown Deer, Wis.: try proposing a wager. "As bankers, we look at past performance. Customers, however, want us to consider future projections - including things like new contracts that will bring higher earnings, or plans to reduce their leverage ratio. We'll say, 'Fine, but if you want us to gamble, you'll have to gamble, too.'"

Here's how it works: let's say the bank is offering prime plus 2%, and you want prime plus 1%. The bank makes the loan at the higher rate, but skims off the amount representing the one-point difference - say, $10,000 - and puts it into an escrow account. If you achieve the agreed-upon projections, you get the money back. For partial achievement, you get a partial return.

And for zero achievement? Not only would you forfeit all that money, but you'd be forced to concede that the banker was, in fact, right in the first place.

READER'S CHOICE
273

Hanging Tough

No bank is going to loan you money unless it is confident of your cash flow and gets enough collateral to protect its investment. So why, on top of that, do most bankers insist on holding you personally liable for the loan? Probably for the same reason they wear belts with their suspenders.

"A bank will always try to get as much protection as it can," says Dan Kolber of Kolber Securities Corp., in Atlanta, who has negotiated dozens of bank loans for various companies, including Air Atlanta Inc., where he was executive vice-president. "But **you should insist on non-recourse debt**" - that is, **debt secured only by collateral**.

If your banker wants you to pledge personal assets, ask why he or she needs the extra security. Isn't the collateral enough? If not, offer more. The banker may say he's worried that something might happen to you. In that case, offer to buy "key man" insurance. Or he may admit that he wants to hold your feet to the fire, at which point you should get huffy. Point to the personal equity you have in the business. If it's not enough, be prepared to put in more.

"Banks will try to intimidate you, but you should hang tough," says Kolber. "I tell them they should be glad to see an owner bargaining hard. If you're not willing to fight for your company, they shouldn't be lending you money."

Insider Information

D o you feel that your banker is holding all the cards when you are renegotiating credit lines and interest rates? According to Evanne Lorraine, you may be able to reshuffle the deck. Lorraine, controller of Daniel Smith, a $10-million art-supply company in Seattle, requests and gets from her bank a monthly analysis of her company's account, which details the bank's costs and profits by type of transaction. "You **know better where there's room to negotiate interest rates and services**," Lorraine says. "It's a case of 'you show me yours, and I'll show you mine.'" Not all banks will share this information, but it's certainly worth a try. Lorraine, for one, has gotten more favorable rates based on knowing the company's value to the bank.

275

Educating Your Banker

If you are having a hard time getting bankers to understand your
business, consider letting a trade magazine do some of the explaining
for you. Mark Winward, CEO of Jane Ink Inc., in Seattle, was in a business
with an image problem: silk-screening and embroidering T-shirts. "All
bankers could think of was sex, drugs, and rock and roll, while I tried to
get them to think of Boeing golf shirts." Sending subscriptions of trade
magazines to prospective and current bankers, Winward says, added an
element of credibility to his appeal that his financials couldn't. The bottom
line? Winward boasts a $500,000 credit line to feed his $3.5 million in sales
per year.

When Loan Officers Come And Go

A common frustration in dealing with banks comes from watching loan officers move on just as you are getting comfortable in the relationship.

While there's little you can do to prevent what sometimes seems a lemminglike migration of bankers, you *can* help cushion the potentially damaging blow to your business. How? **Cultivate a relationship with the junior officer on your account**.

"That's the person likely to be handling the day-to-day activities of your account anyway," says JoAnn Eick, assistant vice-president of Society National Bank, in Cleveland. "If a new senior officer is brought in, you'll have some continuity." And if the junior person is promoted, you'll already be a step ahead as the game starts again.

277

Non credit Check

Growing companies eager to establish a good credit relationship with their bankers often don't **pay attention to the costs of noncredit banking services, such as lock boxes, check reconciliation, and control disbursements**. That can be a costly oversight, as even bankers will admit. "It is in a bank's best interests to insist on a high compensating balance for noncredit services," notes James Sagner, a vice-president in the First National Bank of Chicago's cash-management consulting division. "But that can be very expensive for a small company. Too often, I've seen worries about jeopardizing credit stop a company from questioning overpriced noncredit services."

A case in point is Duncan Oil Co., in Xenia, Ohio. Duncan Oil controller Steve Wells asked the bank for an account analysis statement that broke down their skyrocketing service charges for which the bank insisted on a $100,000 balance in their account to cover the costs. Once Wells received the statement, he immediately opted to pay the service costs rather than keep a high balance. The reason: Wells calculated that by placing money in overnight purchase agreements and other short-term investments, the company could earn $1,800 a month. And Wells says the company's credit line has remained intact.

To fully understand how much noncredit services cost, small companies should formally review their banking charges at least twice a year, says Sagner.

278

Maxing Out

Michael Regan, president of Tranzact Systems, a Chicago-area freight payments service, couldn't figure out why his application for a modest small-business loan kept getting turned down. Then a venture capitalist told him, "Mike, processing a $250,000 credit line and a $750,000 long-term note costs as much as a loan for twice that. Why not make it worth the bank's while?" So, Regan rewrote his application and presto! It was approved.

"**If your cash flow can justify it, make the bank a profitable offer**," advises Regan.

Strength in Numbers

When negotiating with your banker, don't overlook what may be one of your strongest assets - your key executives. If you've invested in these people, why not turn over some of the banking duties to them and impress your banker with your ability to delegate?

That's what Leslie Otten, CEO of Sunday River Skiway Corp., a $23-million ski resort in Bethel, Maine, figured. "For years my banker knew that I was 'it' in the executive suite," says Otten. "That doesn't make a banker feel very comfortable. By 1986 I had assembled a solid team and wanted to let my banker know it." So now, once a year at Sunday River, **the controller and operations and marketing executives take turns meeting with the banker to discuss their departmental plans and performance with him**.

"The banker is pleased to have such substantive contact with my key people," says Otten, who has negotiated loan rates he's happy with. "He sees we have personal approaches but all sing in the same key."

Protecting Your Personal Assets

Don't make the mistake of pledging your personal assets to secure your business loans unless it's absolutely necessary. It often isn't, says one experienced banker we know (who asked to remain anonymous, for fear of retribution from his banker friends). An alternative, he says, is to **get a separate, personal loan and then put the proceeds into the business**. Here's how it works:

Let's say you need a loan of $100,000, and you have equity of $50,000 in your home and an equal amount in the business. The standard bank approach would be to offer you a business loan, backed by the combined equity of your home and business. But, instead, you could ask for two loans, one secured by the house, the other by the business. A first or second mortgage on your home will be much more advantageous from a cash-flow perspective, since business loans are normally written for a 1- to 3-year payback, versus the conventional 30-year term on a home mortgage. And, knock on wood, you won't be out in the cold if anything should happen to the business.

Your banker isn't likely to suggest such an arrangement, but - if you do - he might well go for it. If he doesn't, find another banker who will.

281

Keeping Your Options Open

If your company is growing, you should be preparing right now for the possibility that you'll have to change banks. Most companies don't prepare - and often find themselves without enough credit when they need it most.

To avoid such a predicament, Gordon Jones, of Spectrum Systems Inc., makes a point of staying in touch with a number of banks besides the one that currently handles his company's business. While he has no complaints with his present lender, he realizes that his credit needs are growing along with his business, a Pensacola, Fla., service company that monitors air-pollution levels. "In the past, we've had $100,000 loans on signature. Now we want to be prepared to get a $250,000 loan unsecured, which involves a longer review process."

With that in mind, Jones **sends other banks his financials on a regular basis, so that they'll be acquainted with the business if he ever needs to turn to them for a loan**. "When an opportunity presents itself, I want to be able to take advantage of it," he says, "even if my current bank leaves me out in the cold."

When Your Bank Goes Belly Up

So what *does* happen when a bank slams its door? Thanks to FDIC insurance, a depositor is completely protected up to $100,000. But **a borrower's fate is tied to his prior performance**. If the borrower is current on his loans, the original loan agreements remain in effect whether those assets are purchased by another bank or managed by the FDIC itself. From a cash-flow standpoint, therefore, there's no change. A delinquent borrower, on the other hand, will be required to work out a payment schedule that puts payments on a current basis. And the FDIC has the power to ask for new collateral or additional cosigners.

In short, no borrower is off the hook when a bank goes out of business. "People who think things are forgiven are dreaming," says an FDIC spokesman with a chortle.

283

Spreading the Risks

The recent wave of bank failures has led many companies to take a closer look at how, and where, they invest their idle cash.

One way to minimize the risks of rate-chasing is to diversify. That is the strategy of A. R. Eberhardt, chief financial officer at NetAir International Corp., a Denver-based national air charter network. Eberhardt keeps eight separate $100,000 accounts in banks and savings institutions located in Texas, Arizona, and California.

Of course, this approach only spreads the risk; it doesn't eliminate it altogether. One of the institutions may still go under, taking with it a portion of your corporate cash. Even if the money is insured up to $100,000 per account by the FDIC, it can take months to collect on your losses.

Investors can guard against this possibility by conducting a thorough check of a bank's or S & L's four most recent quarterly statements. Eberhardt himself has developed his own rules of thumb: The institution must be profitable for a year and carry a 3% ratio of net worth to assets. Robert Heady, publisher of *100 Highest Yields*, a financial newsletter in North Palm Beach, Fla., suggests, in addition, that potential investors speak only to the person in charge of national consumer money-market accounts (or whoever would be in charge of handling your business) and "find out how, why, and with whom the bank is loaning money."

Open Communications

If you're like many CEOs, you'd like to make communications between you and your lending institution a two-way street. Terry MacRae, co-founder and principal of Hornblower Yachts Inc., in San Francisco, has found a way: **meet regularly with everyone from your loan officer to the bank president**. Once a quarter the bankers get to see just what their loans are buying, and MacRae gets to check out how *their* portfolio's doing, what management changes are underfoot, and how their short- and long-term plans are coming along.

"When you ask what's new," says MacRae, "it's surprising what they'll tell you." He learned during one meeting that his bank would soon acquire another bank - and he was able to plan an extra cushion of time to process his next loan application.

Don't be afraid to turn the tables and make requests of your bank. "They're selling a service, and you're paying for it," admonishes MacRae. "You have the right to ask for certain things without being bashful."

285

It's All in Who You Know

Conventional business wisdom has it that **accountants are good sources of banking contacts**. Then don't beat around the bush when interviewing potential accounting firms, figured Flo Gillen, CEO of Soft Inc., a computer-programming consulting firm in New York City.

When searching for an accountant, Gillen asked point-blank what kind of banking connections the firm could provide on top of its regular accounting services. While it was only a five-person operation at the time, Soft Inc. was growing rapidly and Gillen needed a credit line fast.

All but one of the accountants she interviewed were vague about what connections they had with banks, says Gillen. "That one was pretty blatant about it," she reports. He offered introductions to bankers he knew at Chase, Chemical, and Citicorp.

Gillen decided to go with his firm and soon had credit lines to choose from. "Sure, it was gutsy, but we needed the money, and it worked," says Gillen, who today employs 40 programmers.

286

"Five years ago
I was ready to get out of business,
to sell my company.
What turned me around was the discovery
that I could use the company
as a tool . . . use it to
promote a cause."

YVON CHOUINARD,
chairman, Patagonia Inc.

Music to Their Ears

Leib Ostrow, CEO of Music for Little People, in Redway, Calif., says he has found a way to increase sales, get favorable publicity, and attract dedicated and like-minded employees. Ostrow **promotes nonprofit organizations "that provide help to the planet" in his mail-order catalog** of cassettes, videotapes, and musical instruments for children.

Customer feedback has been "100-to-1 in favor," Ostrow says. And for at least 3 of the 12 nonprofit groups spotlighted over the past three years, the catalog has been the single most important source of new members.

"These causes are struggling to get started, just like growing businesses. They've had funding cut, and it's up to the entrepreneurs to support them," says Ostrow, whose revenues topped $2 million in 1988.

287

Time Is Money

Clay Teramo is a believer in **giving employees paid time off to do volunteer work**. Though he's still in the process of measuring whatever productivity gains may have resulted from the policy, Teramo says seeing the improvement in morale is enough for him. His $2.7-million company, Computer Media Technology (CMT), in Mountain View, Calif., has 13 employees; on average, one person a week takes an afternoon to volunteer. "We don't want to just give our money away - it's so easily forgotten. And we miss out on the intangible rewards. Volunteering helps keep work from becoming a grind," Teramo says.

For employees who don't have a favorite charity, the company posts a list of local organizations, such as a soup kitchen and a home for the elderly, with a note asking people to give advance notice if they want to help out. "I see it as a win-win situation," says Teramo, who volunteers his own sales and marketing skills for fund-raisers.

Take It Off, All Off

Randy Clark, president of Sun Sportswear Inc., in Kent, Wash., was unpacking T-shirts one day when he realized that **the plastic polybags the company was using for packaging were overkill, *and* they were hurting the environment**.

So in early 1990 the $73-million company started shipping its shirts, tank tops, and sweats right in the box. The clothes arrive less wrinkled since they don't slide around as much, Clark reports, and customers - including Walmart, K mart, and Bradlees - don't miss the plastic.

"It serves the environmental cause," he says, "and it's a cost saver for us." Just how much does it save? At a unit cost of 5¢ per polybag, Sun could wind up saving about $37,500 a year.

289

Organizing a Contest for a Cause

Jacki Baker, co-owner of Mother Myrick's Confectionery & Ice Cream Parlor, an ice-cream shop and mail-order candy business with sales of less than $1 million, **wanted to do something to encourage children to read**.

Baker and her husband, co-owner Ron Mancini, enlisted the help of local high-school art students, who competed to design a game sheet on which grade-school kids could write down the names of books they had read. The winner received a $50 savings bond. Teachers distributed the sheets to 2,000 students in Manchester Center, Vt., and surrounding towns. For each 2 books read, Mother Myrick's would award an ice-cream treat. After reading 11 books, student and family (up to four people) shared a free cake and ice cream.

More than 300 children took part, and the project cost less than $3,000. "Parents told us kids were holed up in their rooms reading," says Baker. Other payoffs were a higher company profile, including a chamber of commerce award, recognition from Vermont governor Madeleine Kunin and First Lady Barbara Bush, and more family visits.

READER'S CHOICE

290

Popped Fresh Daily

Teresa Harrison faced a dilemma. She wanted to assure customers of SET Laboratories Inc. that its packages of software and manuals could be shipped undamaged. But she also **wanted to be kind to the environment by not using polystyrene peanuts for packaging**.

Her solution? Popcorn - which, it turns out, is not only an effective substitute for polystyrene but, aside from the investment of an air popper, costs about 60% less, even if you don't purchase the popcorn in bulk.

The only glitch in using popcorn is that the packaged goods must be enclosed in envelopes, or they will absorb the popcorn smell. Harrison, who founded SET Laboratories in Portland, Ore., three years ago, includes a note explaining the switch and pointing out that, while it is popped fresh daily, the packing material is not intended for human consumption.

I Gave at the Office

Charity solicitation, especially those requests by the typically endless roster of local organizations, is troublesome for many growth-company CEOs. You want to be generous (you may even fear your business's reputation will be harmed if you're not), but you can't afford to give to *everybody*.

Until two years ago, that was the case at Mona, Meyer & McGrath (MMM), a Minneapolis public-relations firm. Then, says CEO David Mona, the company found what it thinks is a solution: **a well-planned, well-stated program for giving**.

MMM gives specified portions of pretax earnings to a few selected organizations, and makes its largest single contribution by taking on one major *pro bono* account each year.

Now, when MMM's managers are pitched by other programs, they can politely say no - citing their policy of committing themselves heavily to one account per year. "It cuts out all the hemming and hawing," says Mona. "We are spending our dollars more wisely and can decline more kindly. We can say, 'Sorry, we've made a decision and we're fully committed in that area.' Not simply, 'We aren't interested,' or, 'We don't care.' They can see we are generous."

Environmentally-Sound Purchasing

At Clean Harbors Inc., a $100-million Quincy, Mass., INC. 100 company that analyzes, cleans up, and transports hazardous waste, **guidelines for purchasing office supplies** include:

*Paper, not Styrofoam, drinking cups
*Biodegradable hand soap for bathrooms
*Recycled paper for stationery

In addition, Clean Harbors forgoes putting salt on the company parking lot after a snowstorm, using only a plow instead.

"The costs associated with these guidelines are negligible in real dollars," says media-relations manager Karen Clancy, "and in many instances actually save money. But the long-term environmental savings are tremendous."

293

Donating Prizes

How do you help solve America's education crisis and get a payback for your company? Jack and Shelly Finnerty, owners of The Pizza Store & More, in Laguna Hills, Calif., do it by rewarding students at a local elementary school.

The Finnertys supply prize certificates for school-sponsored functions, such as paper drives and book-report contests. The prizes happen to be the house specialty, pizza. The pizza may be free, but when students cash in their certificates, soft-drink and other sales also ring up at the restaurant.

"It's inexpensive compared with the payback of motivating students and generating goodwill for our business in the community," says Jack, who figures he's developing a devoted clientele in the process. "As these kids grow up, they'll like my pizza and want to spend their allowances here."

294

Green Card

The environment may be a touchy topic for business executives, but Dick Brooks makes no bones about where he stands on environmental issues. The founder and CEO of a $40-million chemical manufacturing business, ChemDesign Corp., headquartered in Fitchburg, Mass., **prints it right on his business card: "chief environmental officer."**

And it's not lip service. A company subsidiary was named a Friend of the Environment in Wisconsin for cleaning up an old plant it purchased there. Brooks estimates he spends 40% of his time staying ahead of environmental regulations with heavy capital investments in environmental controls.

"It also makes a statement to my employees," says Brooks. "While working at this company you either subscribe to pro-environmental policy or you don't work here."

"I called it that mainly
to embarrass lawyers and accountants.
When they get together
in their dignified offices, they've
got to discuss Poo Poo Pictures.
It's baby talk."

TERRY GILLIAM,
director, Poo Poo Pictures Ltd.,
explaining how he named his company

Sanitizing the Handbook

Don't deprive yourself of an important management tool just because state courts have been treating policy statements in employee handbooks as binding contracts between companies and their employees. **Handbooks can still be an effective means of communicating values and standards, and with careful drafting you can avoid most legal problems**. Here's a checklist from lawyer John Coombe, of Denver-based Holland & Hart:

*Don't include any statement you can't live with - statements "so burdensome on the employer that, in the future, you may not be willing or able to comply."

*Avoid troublesome phrases such as "permanent employee" - they can lead to a dispute over future terminations.

*Don't make strong promises. Instead of stating the company "will provide" or "will guarantee" something, say "the company will, whenever practical, provide." Avoid using "guarantee" altogether.

*Don't say that employees will be fired only "for cause." List all the reasons for firings. Many employers go so far as to include disclaimer language reserving the right to discharge at any time for any reason.

*At the beginning and the end of the handbook include a disclaimer to the effect that "this is not a contract. It can be modified at any time."

*Review the handbook regularly and eliminate outdated rules.

Battling the Gray Market

f you subcontract with a foreign manufacturer, the gray market may be a threat to your business. But now, thanks to a recent U.S. Supreme Court ruling, you can help protect yourself by 1) carefully wording your agreement with the subcontractor, and 2) registering with the U.S. Customs Service.

Unlike counterfeit black-market goods, which are manufactured illegally, gray-market goods are legally produced but distributed in unauthorized ways. If, for example, a foreign company has sold you its trademark for exclusive use in the United States, then tries to compete with you here by distributing the product itself, that product is a gray-market import.

Here's how you can help Customs guard your interests by blocking the product at the border. First, be sure that your relationship with the overseas manufacturer is contractually defined as licensee/licensor - if you're affiliated with the gray marketer as either parent or subsidiary, Customs won't protect you. And remember to let the Customs Service in on your arrangement: record your trademark with it.

297

Law

The Subsidiary Shield

If one part of your business carries greater liability risk than others, you may be able to protect the rest of your company by spinning it off as a separate corporation**. But be careful: the new subsidiary must be a truly independent corporation. That means:

*It must function independently in its day-to-day operations.

*It must have sufficient capital of its own to carry on its business.

*It must have the authority to act in its own best interests, even if they conflict with those of the parent company.

*Customers and other outsiders must understand that the corporations are separate entities and must know which one they're dealing with.

*Each corporation must observe all the formalities of federal, state, and local laws, as well as its own by-laws.

Of course, would-be plaintiffs may still sue the parent as well as the subsidiary. But, provided you follow the rules, the courts will generally respect the subsidiary as a real legal entity and a viable shield for other parts of your business.

298

Guerrilla Contracts

S teep legal fees for writing an international contract didn't stop Bill Olschewski, CEO of Apex Microtechnology Corp., in Tucson, from taking on the world when his company was but a start-up seven years ago. To enter the global market, Olschewski wrote his own agreements. "We got a sample for an international distributor contract from another company in a similar situation and based ours on it. Just use some of the same language and translate it to fit your own requirements," Olschewski recommends. He **still writes his own contracts** even though sales are up to $7 million a year - 30% of that from abroad.

299

The Value of Being Precise

I t may be inconvenient, or expensive, to put agreements into precise contracts, but do it anyway. **Vague contracts can come back to haunt you, plunging your company into major legal wrangles down the road. They can also reduce the value of your business**.

So says Randall Wise, the man responsible for evaluating acquisition candidates for Lotus Development Corp. Time and again, he says, deals have to be killed or prices lowered because the acquiree has vague contracts. "It costs money to clean things up," he notes, and that cost is reflected in the acquirer's final valuation.

Some of the problems that Wise often sees in the companies he looks at:

*oral agreements that have never been reduced to writing;

*lack of a termination date;

*unspecified commitments to provide service for a product; and

*failure to specify what happens when the contract is breached.

If you can't afford the legal expense of drafting every agreement, have a lawyer develop boilerplate contract language. "The first three times you use it, you will see how your customers react," Wise says. After working with the lawyer to revise the language, you should be able to go it alone.

Protecting Your Client Base

I f you run a professional service business, you're probably not surprised when employees leave and take their - and your - clients with them. Happens all the time, but it's troublesome nonetheless. Norman Ochelski, who operates his own CPA firm in Detroit, has a solution: **require new hires to sign a contract stating they will pay the going market rate for clients that they swipe**.

"I can't force a client to stay with my company when one of my CPAs moves on; after all, client relationships can get pretty close. But I do get fair payment when it happens," Ochelski says. He typically receives one and a quarter times the account's yearly gross billings when a CPA takes the business out the door. "Usually it's between one and two times depending on where the business is located. It's an agreement that stands up in court because the employer would be incurring financial hardship - it's based on what the practice would sell for [on the open market]."

Ochelski has never been taken to court on the agreement, but a friend has, and he won his case. "It's not as common as it should be, given how fair and easy to implement it is. This way there are no hard feelings when we part company."

READER'S CHOICE

301

Other *Inc.* Publishing
publications include:

**How to Really Start Your
Own Business**
By David E. Gumpert

**How to Really Create a
Successful Business Plan**
By David E. Gumpert

**The Anatomy of a Start-Up:
27 Real-Life Case Studies**
*Why Some New Businesses Succeed
Where Others Fail*
Edited by
Elizabeth K. Longsworth

Inc. Magazine's **IDEA SWEEPSTAKES**

Do you think you have management ideas like the ones found in this book that set your company apart? Then send them in. We challenge companies across the country to compete in submitting the most innovative ideas to solve management dilemmas.

The company that submits the best ideas overall, as judged by a panel of _Inc._ editors, will have their ideas as well as a picture of the entire company published in _Inc._ magazine. In addition, Tom Peters will extend a free admission for one at his management "Skunk Camp".

So share this with your colleagues, compete with other divisions, turn it into a companywide contest. Have fun. Simply fill out the form below and write up a brief description of each idea (use extra sheets if necessary.) The deadline date for applications is February 15, 1992.

Company Name: _____

Address: _____

Phone: _____

Business Description: _____ Number of Employees: _____

Publicly or Privately Held: _____ Total Revenues: _____

Your Name: _____

Your Position/Department: _____

IDEAS:
(Use additional sheets if necessary)

Send entry form to:
Inc. Idea Sweepstakes,
Inc. magazine,
38 Commercial Wharf,
Boston, MA 02110-3883.